7,001 RESUMES,

THE JOB

ABOUT THE AUTHORS

Gene Merhish is a college, adult education, and high school instructor with over twelve (12) years of teaching experience. Trained in Business Education and recognized as a Business Education Consultant for the State of California, he operated one of the most advanced programs in the teaching of retailing merchandising in the Western States. In addition, Mr. Merhish has over twenty-six (26) years of business and marketing experience with such companies as Proctor and Gamble, Gardner-Denver, Harnischfeger Corporation, Accurate Air Engineering, and past president of an entrepreneurial corporation. Mr. Merhish has more than 15 years of military experience with the Navy, Air Force Reserves, and National Guard. He also serves as a business and marketing teacher at Ivy University, Alhambra, California, and several junior colleges. He also works in consort with China Training Center For Senior Civil Servants, Ministry of Personnel, and The People's Republic of China. In addition, Mr. Merhish works with small businesses as a marketing and sales consultant.

Dr. Robert Dussman is a former Navy officer who served in various elite units including the famed UDT/Seal Teams and 1st Anglico. He worked as an aerospace engineer for over twenty years with such companies as Boeing, Douglas Aircraft and Northrop. Dr. Dussman holds a BA, MBA, JD, and three years of post doctorate education. Dr. Dussman does outside financial consulting to small business and private parties. He is currently a computer teacher in a Southern California School District.

HOW TO USE THIS BOOK

7,001 RESUMES, THE JOB SEARCH WORKBOOK guides you step-by-step through the process of developing and excuting a job search and career development plan.

The best way to use this book is to start with Chapter One Introduction. Introduction will give you the opportunity to get your bearing and determine your current position. It will also give you an idea of how we proceive the challeges facing the job searcer. Armed with this knowledge, you can progress quickly through the book and start advancing your career and finding that next position.

We provide employment references. Many of these resources are available at your local or university libraries. We also provide potencial employers and organizations that you might consider for possible employment.

This is a job search workbook it is designed for you to write in it as you do yourself evaluation, and refer to it throughout your career. Many chapters include additonal worksheets. Samples have been completed in this book to show you information the employer is looking for. Remember the information is designed to help you evaluate what you have to offer a potencial employer and assist you in presenting the information in away that will put you in the best light.

ACKNOWLEDGEMENTS

It must be acknowledged that to accomplish any task, it takes dedication, perseverance, teamwork, and cooperation. I would like to thank my with Bobbie, step-daughter, Brianna, and son-in-law Kirk, for all their patience and understanding.

Bob is appreciative of the patience and understanding he received from his wife Valerie and son Bobby, who put up with us while we were writhing and developing this book.

Published by Camelsealbooks, DBA

C 1998

Manufactured and Printed in the United States of America

Table Of Contents

   Your introduction to the real world of job search starts here. This workbook
   will assist you in developing ideas, theories, and concepts to help you obtain
   your next job.

   This chapter introduces you to the concepts of supply and demand and how
   supply and demand can influence your job opportunities.

   You will find in this chapter how effectiveness and efficiency interrelate.

   To set yourself apart from the pack, and we can assume there is a pack out
   there; you may have to do something unique. This chapter addresses some
   unique approaches.

   What tracking is and how you can use it.

   The concept of career planning and how to formulate possible career strategies.

Introduction

The purpose of this book is to discuss some of the real trials and tribulations of a job search, and more importantly explore how you "**really**" get a job today in these uncertain times use our experience, ideas, observations, inventories, planning, and information gathered from many other sources over the years. This information come from all over the country from many levels within various organizations. Use this book as a "tool", a workbook to build the ammunition to win the battle of getting that job. This is one of the most important battles of your life.

A person used to work for one company or organization for their entire working career of about forty-five years. This is no longer true. There is little to no loyalty by companies to the workers, and the companies should expect to get none back from the employees. An employee who is will downsized, rightsized, re-organize, and fire em-ployees when times get hard or there are changes in the market, be it na-tional or for-eign, to gain a few profit points. They expect to pick up "new" qualified employees as they need them in the future with little to no regard for the employee's economic situation or the employee's family. This all done in the name of saving, money, re-organization, progress, or whatever the popular "buzz" word is at the time.

Companies justify this in the eternal drive for more money in profits for the shareholder not to mention higher and higher bonuses for the top executives. Organization feel if they fail to do this, someone else will. This "Darwin Capitalism" gone mad! It feeds on itself to destruction! Firms feel they either make more money or go out of business. The world is becoming an even more competitive place. The world is getting smaller and companies believe that they must not only compete with business from around the corner but from around the world. Companies are cutting corners everywhere, and if you are reading and planning to use this book, you may be a "victim" of this process. This process results in higher prices and less service. Gas stations used to check your oil, wash your windows, fill your car up with gas and give you stamps. Nobody does this today and it seems that service is as "dead" as the dinosaur. Today, the indications are that companies will cut service anywhere they can to increase or protect their profits if they believe that they are in jeopardy; be it fact or fictions.

Efficiency is the name of the game today. The more efficient you are, the more money the "bigger" you get. This usually comes at the expense of the employee or the customer (or both). The "Key" question for most people is how do you adjust to the "new" world of cold reality in which every one is out to get whatever they can at the expense of others. This may be a bit cynical, but it often seems true. This is the "real" world we face each day now and into the future. You must be wary these days. We know of a friend who was happily retired for nearly ten (10) years. He and his wife thought they had it made! One day one of this five children's husband was "downsized" and guess who was back in the job market? Always keep you resume' up-to-date. You never know what will happen next.

The managers today are mainly interested in protecting their "fat" pay checks, bonuses and benefits. They do not care mainly the "new" workers who must learn to do their jobs themselves or be fired. The managers cannot train them because they do not know the jobs. They never will know or understand the jobs.

You may feel your termination was unfair. This may or may not be true. Most people do not have the money to fight a lawsuit. The companies always have unlimited resources and attorneys on call to handle lawsuits. The company usually win the lawsuits anyway. You are losing time. No income is coming in. You may be included on an unpublished "Black List" of trouble-making employees that employers may not want working for them. These "Black lists" are available on the internet to any employer willing to pay for them. The employer wants to know if you are going to make trouble for them: once on a "Black List", an employee may have a difficult time getting off.

the truth is, you may never get off this list. Black list may be legal if they only contain factual information on which employees have sued the former employers. This is seldom done. The lists are used to assure a given employee will never work again.

The usual Black List lawsuits against a company for "bad" conduct are almost always worthless. The company can lay a person off for any reason or no reason. An organization will usually make up a reason (other than the real reason) if no other reason comes to mind.

Companies are ing the real rea- shown the door.

getting very clever at disguis- son why workers are being

One company dark-skinned reason and won ployee who company because was un- left. The reason are aware of a has suggested his administra- group. Does not mean you you should give

recently downsized an older, employee for apparently no a lawsuit brought by the em- sued for discrimination. The claimed he was "downsized" able to do the work that was was due to his skin color. We School Superintendent who that he wants to replace all of tors with a specific ethnic this go on you bet! This does do not have a chance or that up. No, it means that you

need to be aware on what really goes on in the "real" world of job search.

Older workers are particularly vulnerable to the trend toward downsizing, of staff reduction. Older workers who earn say 60K a year with benefits are being replaced by three (3) workers for 21K a year with no benefits for the first year. This apparently has been a national trend since we can see the high numbers of employees over 50 years old being laid off both sexes, and various ethnic groups. This same group overwhelmingly is having extreme difficulty finding worthwhile employment to match their experience and education levels. We not only see this in business and industry, but in the Education Community.

This type of thinking ignores the fact that no work will get done because there is no one left who knows how to do the job. The seasoned, laid-off employees get frantic phone calls at home from the "new" hires to find out what is going on or how to do their job. Or the seasoned certificated individual may be call by a desperate school district to substitute, but no full-time job offers.

The management people who laid off seasoned people are supposed to know what is going on but they do not. The companies discover (too late) what was to be a money-saving idea more often than not costing these firms and organizations a great deal more than if they had kept their original employees. They would have continued to do the job and make money, or get the job done without delay or disruption. (Not to mention the added cost of hiring, firing, and other related administrative costs.)

The employee should always have a "current" resumes' and a letter of introduction at all time. If you are in Education you will always need three (3) current letters of recommendation when applying for a position. Remember it is always easier to get a job while you are working. Do not wait until you get a "Pink Slip" or a lay-off notice to start a job search. This is a big mistake. Any individual should always be out looking for the "next" opportunity or career growth situation. Remember there is little to no "loyalty" by the company or organization today. You will want to be careful with the degree of loyalty you give in return. Some suggest that it can be very "foolish", to be too loyal these days. We would not suggest that it is "foolish", but be careful. There are good businesses, school districts, government positions, and organization out there however, they are many times over-shadowed by many bad ones. Good organizations are like the bald eagle, they are in short supply. A person can never tell about the organization until it is to late.

A person can expect on an average to get seven lay-off notices in a forty-five (45) year career. The average person will change careers at least four (4) times during a lifetime. A change of career means to start a job that an individual has never done before. This may mean a major change in salary (generally downward) or it could mean an increase if your experience can be used in the new fields. Most people starting a career are not aware of these facts. It is "never" taught in school. Rarely does anyone discuss this with new employees.

Individuals should always be involved in career training to go into new fields like computers and the internet if there appears to be upward possibilities in those areas. Eighty-five (85) percent of new career changes require some type of additional schooling or vocational training. This takes hard work and commitment! The employee should always take advantages of employer-paid training opportunities or pay for training if the employer does not provide this benefit. Employee training can be obtained nearly everywhere these days.

People should move toward jobs that appears to be in demand. New jobs are created all the time. Old jobs fall by the wayside. For example, firemen in the railroad industry, gas station attendants, and blueprint checkers in the aerospace industry, these were all once important jobs that have been replaced by changes in workplace. This is supply and demand at work. It is nothing personal. Jobs can (and do) come and go all the time.

365 days a year. No one has any more or any less time.. The "key" to success is what you do with the limited amount of time you have. You are the only person who can control what you do with your time. It is your time while you are alive. It is like money in your pocket. You may choose to spend it as you like. You should spend it wisely. Invest in yourself first. Like the story of the ants and the grass-hopper, the grasshopper watched and joked as the ants gathered food, then came the day that the grasshopper was hungry and he had no stored food to fall back on, but the ants who used their time wisely had gathered food for the "rainy day" and did not have to worry about be-   ing hungry. Are you an ant or the grasshopper.

The highest-priced worker are those that do very little physical work. They are the workers who "think", "plan", "speak", "manage", "control", and "direct." Thinking is one of the most highly prized and least understood functions in the economy. There are many common misunderstandings about those who think for a living.

The person who digs ditches for a living can get tired physically from his work. The "mind" worker will never get physically tired because the mind cannot get tired. The mind may get   bored but it can never get tired. The mind is available for work at any   time the person is awake. The mind also offers solutions in dreams while   we sleep.

The most im-   portant person to any economy is the "mind" worker. The more you   think, the better worker you are. The better worker you are the more   money you will make. This is a cycle that will repeat itself again and   again. The highest paid workers are those who think the best. Non-thinking workers usually do not rise to great levels in any organization. They are quickly replaced by smarter thinking people.

It is important to work smarter not harder. The best work you can do   re-quires the least effort and the most creativity. It requires you to look at   what you are doing and think of ways to improve things. The most impor-   tant worker to an organization is the employee who thinks and asks him-   self the key question, "What can I do to make more money for myself and   be more profitable for my company?" These workers are few and far be-   tween. You may know some of them. They are the rising stars, the ones that go the "extra" mile.

Thirty years ago, the workforce represented 20 percent college grads, 70 percent manual la-borers, and 10 percent technical people. Thirty years from now, there will still be a need for 20 percent college graduates, 79 percent technical people but less than 1 percent for manual laborers. The growth area will be for people with at least some technical training. Manual

labor will be almost entirely gone! Education will be key to the future (especially technical education).

In America we must focus also on competition from a global work force we must prepare for the excelling information Age, an era dominated by technology and knowledge, as well as globalization. By 2005, almost half of U.S. workers well be in industries related to information technology. Already, the leading job category in U.S. labor statistics is computer and data processing. The fastest growing occupations required the most education and are concentrated in the business-services and health-services industries. This is much different from the last century, when highly educated professions such as doctors and lawyers represented such a small percentage of the job market.

Those talented professionals will have more opportunities to work from their home relying on the Internet, computer power and faster broadband speeds. With more people working from home there will be more opportunities for door-to door sales.

We will see a rising rate of the re-hiring of retirees to teach remedial math and reading programs as well as teach customer service. We will also see more women making inroads into managerial and executive ranks. Today, the number of women earning four-year college degrees has surged 44 percent since 1979 now represent 56 percent of the estimated 1,140,000 college graduates reports the Department of Education.

Another booming area of opportunity will be financial and retirement planning as the nearly 77 million baby boomers begin to hit 65 in 2011.

Ex-retail workers will flood the job market as competition from catalogs and online centers will force many retail stores to close. They will compete for jobs in marketing and sales, making those sectors fiercely competitive.

Employees will become increasingly isolated, relying on digital communication rather than face-to-face interaction. If social skills diminish, this could hinder collaboration and threaten productivity. So it is safe to say that in order to stay competitive one needs to maintain not only social skills, but to also continue training and developing technical skills that will keep you competitive into the 21st century and beyond. Surely the **"key"** to career success is Education and training!

Chapter Three

Effectiveness vs Efficiency

It is important for you to understand the difference between effectiveness and efficiency. It is also important to understand how effectiveness and efficiency play out at the company you were (are) working for and the one you are going to.

Effectiveness means that you are doing the right things. Efficiency means you are doing the most amount of work for the least amount of money. You are getting the most **"bang for your bucks."** Both you and your company must be both effective and efficient or there will be major problems. You may be effective by doing the right thing. You are following this book so you are probably doing the right things in order to get a job. You have to keep trying until you are successful.

You have to be efficient also by conducting cost effective programs. Your money is limited. You have to evaluate what responses you are getting to get the most out of them. Do not continue methods that have failed or that you feel uncomfortable with. You are **"captain of your own ship."** You have to keep the ship off the rock pile.

The com- pany that recently "downsized" you (or that you are not happy with) probably believes they can get someone for less money or that your job can be eliminated. A company will not keep an employee for 80K a year with benefits if they feel they can hire three (3) new college graduates for 20K with no benefits for the first year. You are "damned" if you do and "damned" if you do not. You are either over- qualified or un-qualified for the job. This is something that you are going to have to contend with as you interview for your next position.

You want to get more money but more money may make you the next one to go.

Here is the problem. A company may not hire you as a new employee for 80K a year because it is too much, but on the other hand, if you agree to go to work for 20K, they more than likely will not hire you because they know that as soon as you find a better-paying position, you will leave. They will have wasted money training you only to find they must find someone to replace you if they do hire you for the lower salary and you leave.

The company will always try to do the right things by being in the right industry and bringing the right product to market. A firm will go broke if it fails to do this. The business wants to retain the best possible employees at the least possible wages. This ensures that the organization can make the maximum profit for the owners and stockholders. This also ensures the maximum bonus for the company's executives. "Greed" is everywhere. Some people believe greed is good, and others practice the concept.

The company must be effective and efficient or it will go out of business quickly. A competitor will do the right things to force the company's hand. The "wolves" are at the door. All people (and companies) must compete or be wiped out. This is the law of business today.

A person must always be looking for opportunity in the ever-changing climate of business today. The firm will seldom tell the employee where the opportunity lies. The company will also seldom tell the employees about future downsizing plans. The reason for this is the good employees would look elsewhere for work and bad employees would be downsized anyway. Either way, the company loses. Politically, no bosses/managers want to tell employees that in six (6) months they will be "downsized." The boss/managers will wait until the last possible minute and then blame someone else even if they are the ones responsible for the downsizing. The bosses/manager will always take credit when things go right but avoid taking blame if things go wrong. This is like many politicians.

This will leave most employees in the dark most of the time. The smart employee should always be ready to go out the door at a moment's notice. You should not be in a "**panic**," but as they say in the Boy Scouts, **"Be Prepared."** Have your feelers out at all times. Be aware of what is out there in the marketplace. Float your resume out to your industry all the time because you never know when the "ax" will fall. It is always too late when you find out! Go to trade shows (if possible) to see what the competition is doing and make contacts if the ax falls your way.

A smart employee will always keep his/her letters of introduction and resume up-to date. Some would argue that these are disloyal acts or being a dishonest employee. We would say that in today's world, they are "smart, good, enterprising, creative, and aware" employees. The company by-in-large has little to no loyalty to you today and you would be "foolish" if you give much back to the firm. You should do your job. You can be assured that your company would lay you off as soon as times get bad or change. You only have to consult the business section of your local newspaper to confirm this fact. We have said this again and again.

Remember, the "big shots" at these companies will always get their high salaries as they are "rightsizing" you out the door and sending you to the unemployment line. They will have no pity on you. You will be told that you will be hired back as soon as times get better. They will not miss a paycheck. You may be hearing the "we will be here when you get back speech," but this may never happen. This may seem cynical, but do not trust anyone. Always check everything out yourself and then proceed with what you think is correct. You should be looking all the time for a new job or a better position. Test the waters to see what is out there. Remember, you do not have to jump or take another positions. Now you have more power. Knowledge is power!

Once you are "downsized", your whole interest should be geared up to what is best for you and what you need to do to get another job. You can expect to get little real help from anyone. You are on your own. We hate to break the news to you this way, but if you want to get another job, you are going to do all the work. You have been give the kiss of death. No one will want to be with you, or even know you at this point in time.

Your "new" firm will be looking for your help to do the right things (effectiveness) and doing the right thing as cheaply as possible (efficiency). You have to show them you will do this at the time of the interview. They must believe you are the right person for them.

It is important to convince the new employers that you can (and will) add something new to the company to help them to solve whatever the problems are that they have. You must "add value"   for them.

Show them      you will "fit in" to their organization while
you are doing   all these great things for them. They must be
convinced   you can and will do the job. You must be a
"salesman"   selling the most important product that there
is. This is   you! Many applicants do not realize this or do
not want to   admit it, but you are a product or commodity.
You must   sell yourself! No one else will.

CHAPTER FOUR

Specialty Approaches To Job Search

You may find it hard to get a job. Statistics tell us that in today's economy, you are fortunate to get one interview out of over 100 attempts. Your range will vary. as an example, an applicant had an inside lead that a 100 million dollar California company was looking or would be looking for a marketing manager. Now for several reasons, the applicant wanted this position. Remember, all of us have many motivations as to why we want to work for a company. These reasons are influenced by economic conditions, need, ego, location, money or whatever. This company in question offered the applicant a good income, good location and the applicant saw some challenges.

Well, the applicant did the traditional thing. He sent the resume and cover letter. He made the follow-up phone call but to no avail. He sent his package to several people within the organization. So the next step, since he really wanted to interview, was to come up with some 'gimmick' to get the attention of the president. So he decided to design a five foot long poster with his computer wishing him a Merry Christmas. Of course, it was in color and he felt it was well done.

The result! I would like to say that the President was impressed, and he called the applicant to offer him the position. Not true. The applicant never heard from him. Anyway, not only did he not get an interview, he got no acknowledgement for his innovative approach in getting some recognition from the President. If nothing else, a thank you for the holiday banner. The message here is try anything! He did set himself apart from the others. He was sure no one else had done this before, at least not at this company. Remember, we have decided that there are two kinds of employers, one that will hire you and one that will not. This President did not recognize creativeness and could not relate it to the needs of his company. Maybe someone else would.

Anyone can send resumes. True creativity is hard to come by.

You may fax, E-mail, or send telegrams to express your interest in a company. You may use designed newsletter found here in the workbook, mini-marketing plans for firms to show your creativity and skills to capture a position. Within the last two years, you may have seen employment ads requesting that you design a mini-marketing plan along with the cover letter, application, resume, and salary history. This is the wave of the future. It is somewhat a pretest for you, it screens out some candidates who are not serious about the position, or who do not have the skills. It may work. You should give it a try.

Today, you see the need to be able to use a second and third language. It is to your advantage to take courses in other languages in order to enhance your skills and qualifications. Some positions require a second language and other suggest that it would be a good idea to know a second language.

This is the same with becoming computer 'savvy'. This fact cannot be overemphasized. Computer skills will set you apart, providing the potential employer with a candidate with varied skills. You will want to have as varied skills as possible. The employer wants to get the most 'bang for his buck.' You will want to be able to offer as many skills as possible.

You may prepare a job description which discusses your duties and compensation sheet outlining in detail how much you want to make, which should include expenses and all related compensation and benefits. You should be able to sit down with an employer and go over this document line by line. Some managers are impressed and others will not be.

Job hunting is a good example of the old Boy Scout motto, 'Be prepared.' You should be ready for anything, especially the curve balls the interviewer may throw your way. You must be flexible.

CHAPTER FIVE

Tracking

Tracking is a concept that may be new to some of you. You may recognize the term "pigeon-holed." The basic rule if tracking is that once you enter a "track," it is difficult if not impossible to get out of it.

You may be tracked in many different ways but most people are tracked in at least two different ways. These are by job type and company type.

You can chose what track you are on but you should choose carefully. Especially if you can move early in your working career. Human relations departments always want you to return to your track because it is easier for them. You may or may not want to go back to where they think you should be. Once you are a welder it may be difficult for human relations to recognize that you have attributes that would allow you to be a benefit to the firm in the Marketing department.

The first question is, "Do you want to be in a large or small organization?" There are advantages and disadvantages to both. A large organization can offer you a higher salary and better benefits than a small organization. The large organization can also offer better support resources to get the job done. On the other hand, the large organization can be cold and impersonal. It may even be hostile especially if you later discover the job to be a bad fit for you.

A small organization may give you a better overview of what is going on. You may get experience un a large number of areas as opposed to the pigeon-holing that can go in at the large corporation. The job may seem more interesting because you are doing a variety if jobs. You can move quickly from job to job. If you opt to go to work for the small firm, you may be the Marketing Manager, Advertising Manager, and may even have an opportunity to get involved in product development and manufacturing. This kind of experience may have many benefits to you throughout your career

You may be able to move up faster in a small organization because everyone would know that you are doing a great job. You may have a more important role from the start. A small organization may be less bureaucratic, less political than a large organization.

On the other hand, a small company may give you experience that is a mile wide and an inch deep. You may not be able to move to a large organization once you are tagged as a small company person. Large organizations want people with a lot of experience in one small area. This can be frustrating.

You may also may find that in the small firm often family members are integrated within the firm. This can thwart promotional oppor-  tunities. Promotions or management positions may automati- cally go to these members regardless of their abil- ity or attitude.

The next key decision for you is what area to go into. Be careful on this one. There are a lot of areas you might like. Most people take the first job they are offered and wind up staying there for their entire career. The reason for this is that it is hard to move from being say a salesperson to a production manager as the company may want you to stay in sales. Your best bet is to try some type of management trainee program and rotate through different areas before you select one for your career. You probably want to do this early in your career.
The most significant thing is to look at all the advantages and disadvantages for each area before you set down roots in any one area as you may be there for a long time.

Remember. once you are tracked it may be hard to change to another area once you gain experience. You may want to move but be unable to get a job where you want to be. Tracking can either help you get a new job or it can destroy any chance you may have had to get a new job. You should always endeavor to use tracking to your advantage when you are out looking for work.

Re- like for the not be chance member to tell the interviewer that this potential job is the other jobs you have had. This will make it easier employer to see that the transition to the new job will too difficult. At the same time it will give you a better to get the new position.

CHAPTER SIX

Career Planning

Career planning is somewhat of an "oxymoron" in today's world. There is no real career planning since the opportunity may vary quickly. You should try to do some long-range planning ti see how you are doing against your own plan. Your best plans may 'go up in smoke' at a moment's notice so you must be flexible. You must 'adapt ' or 'die.' Like the dinosaur, if you fail to adapt, you too are gone. The quicker you do the job, the better off you will be and the faster you will recover from being unemployed. Unemployment can bring a loss if face as well as money. It can lead to all sorts if problems, including death.

Truly, opportunities are everywhere and at the same time, no where; they are like the mirrors In the fun house at the museum park. You may see them but you might find yourself bumping into many other mirrors before you find the right path to follow. You should not turn down any opportunity to talk with anyone at any time that might be willing to help you. Always go to the interview even if you must schedule it for after hours or weekends. You never know what will happen or what might be offered. You do have the right to say 'no' once a job is offered. It is not necessary that you accept every offer or any offer for that matter. The job should fit you and your needs. The author has turned down several teaching and business positions due to the need to relocate which would have caused undue stress on the family as well as economic considerations. It is important to know how far you are will-ing to commute (or move) to get a job. A job may be 'GUD' (geographically undesirable) but it may have other things that are worthwhile (like pay). You will never know unless you go to the interview to see what is offered. Some employers may allow you to telecommute (work at home by computer) 2 or 3 days a week. This can cut down your traveling

Your employer may give you additional education opportunities and training at his expense. You will want to be sure that you take full advantage of any of these offerings. You will never know when this training will benefit you in a future career move outside your present, and there is no question it will be helpful within your company of employment. If your em-ployer will pay for Adult Education, Junior College or University courses, take full advan-tage of this opportunity also. You may not have this opportunity on your next job. We have said this once and we will continue to repeat it over and over, "knowledge is power". In today's economy as we continue see new technologies come on the scene and old ones disappear more and more quickly, it is prudent to continue to expand your education to stay competitive in the market place.

You should try to expand your knowledge of "cross-training" if it is available. Cross-training may include areas you like as hobbies. You may be able to do a hobby as a full-time job. Your vocation can be an avocation. You should do the best you can to attempt to "cross-train" to other departments. This will give you more experience and make you a more valuable employee. It may also give you a greater contacts and options in case something goes wrong on your current job. This is great opportunity to do **networking** on the job.

The more people you know, the better off you are. More jobs are gotten by networking than being out there sending out resumes and trying to job search.

Our recommendation to you is to continue to go to school the rest of your life. This is what we suggest to all our students at the college level as well as at the high school level. You will be a better person for it. Of course, we can only suggest and recommend you will have to be the one who make the final decision and commitment is up to you, but you will be the one who benefits from the commitment.

Most smart managers have deals like this. They are called "recips." The deal is if I get laid off in my department, you will pick me up in your department and visa versa. Both managers are sure the other will help. Some Managers have "recips" with lots of other managers in their company or elsewhere. "Recips" are more common the higher you go. No high manager wants to be out "pounding" the streets looking for work. "Recips" are harder to get for lower level employees, but try to get one if you can. Recips are always a great deal for both parties. You should always be ready to use one if need be. You never know what will happen next. Change will always occur at the worst possible time for your Always be prepared.

CHAPTER SEVEN

Your Assets

Ok, now get out the notebook or sheet of paper. Do this for you, not because we tell you to. The following is to be used in the development of your cover letter, resume, newsletter, follow-up, and the interview. We want to take some time and write down what you believe you have to offer a company. People almost always under-value what they have and can give to a company. Believe us, the most important asset to most companies is people. There is a quotation to this effect somewhere. You face serious competition. We would say to our students when we teach adult education and high school as well as our employees, to look around. You are in competition with students in your class as well as other schools within the city, older adults returning to the work force, and of course college students.

Like the high school students, you are
tion with a lot more people than you
ize. You are in competition from the
population, but you are also in competi-
ployees within the organization, institu-
ness, or company. You may be in com-
friends, relatives, and friends of people
the company you have selected as your
work. So you must get a grasp of your
member, there is always competition
worthwhile job including working for
Competition is a fact of life. Competi-
Competition will not go away. It is
can use it to your advantage. It can
land your ideal job.

in competi-
my first real-
general
tion with em-
tion, busi-
petition with
working for
next place of
assets. Re-
for any
yourself.
tion is good.
there and you
help you to

One more thing, I want you to think about, what does the second place applicant earn in the job interview? Nothing! You will want to be the first place winner in the job interview, this means you must beat out all the other competition. That is if you want to work at the place you selected as your next place of employment.

This is a list you can use: (please fill in with your own information)

Business assets:

General Management

Manufacturing

Personnel/Human Resources

Marketing

Finance & Accounting

Procurement

Research & Development

Packaging

Administration

International Operations

Etc., Etc

Under each one of these categories, you will indicate your function and experience. In front if you have experience (business or personal), place a "+".
Next, place a double plus "++" in front of each function for which you would like to be responsible in your next position. Place a triple plus "+++" in front of the functions you want to be involved with on a hands-on/day-to-day bases. (minimum of 3, maximum of 5)

The key is to know what you have to offer!

You should also list your functions and discuss with an associate or friend. Have them circle words that most closely describe your primary experiences and background. You will also want to circle the words that you feel describe your experiences and background and compare.

Example:

Sales	Organizational Management
Sales Management	Financial Management
Manufacturing Engineering	Senior Management
Engineering	Marketing
Communication	General Management
Senior Executive Management	Graphic Design
Management	Computer Applications

You can add More Items

Accomplishments, Duties, Experience, and Background

We now want to list and circle each work that describes your overall accomplishment, duties, experiences, and background.

Example:

Financial	Projects	media
MISS	design	promotion
operations	proposals	project
management	negotiations	administration
franchise	start-up	training & development
public relations	analysis	electronics
liaison	purchasing	business development
account executive	manufacturing	business development
sales	import	user interface
research	franchise operations	sales training
account retention		

You Can Add More Items

Jobs will disappear if it is not required or is replaced by technology. The computer has replaced many jobs but opened up a lot of new careers. Many computer-related jobs did not exist a few years ago.

Our job searching experience transcends more than three decades and numerous positions with small, medium, national, international-sized firms in several industries as well as in the educational community. Our experience spans (60) years with companies like Boeing, Douglas Aircraft, Lockheed Missiles & Space Company, Northrop, Proctor and Gamble, Gardner-Denver, Harnischfeger, Deustch, and to name of few. We have also taught over twenty (20) years (between the two of us) at all levels of education.

We have been working a long time, and have done numerous jobs like many people of our age. We are sure that you have heard this story before, and you may even tell the story to your grandkids. We have served in the military, been a caddy, pumped gas, and worked for a 'carnie' at the end of each summer for several years during the Iowa State Fair. We have been on a job search most of our lives as we seek upward mobility or to combat the "gauntlet" of downsizing, rightsizing, and the like. We have 'been there' a few times over the years.

We have had between us more than fifty jobs during our career some we wanted and others we took because we were unemployed. Downsizing isn't new, just a new "buzz" term like "rightsizing", and "pruning". Like you, we have been "pruned", "downsized", and "rightsized". The truth is, we are continuing our job searching now. We are trying to recover our "top" level jobs. Both of us have full-time teaching positions but are working toward Administration positions and teaching again at the college and university level. This book is to help you get a job. It is a reflection of the dynamic changes in the work environment. These changes will continue to evolve regardless of who is in the White House. These changes are driven by the economy itself. Any "ripple" in the economy may be a "tidal wave" to you. To be more precise this book is going to be an up-to-the minute, "what is "happening now," work book.

So if you will take some time and read, believe that we not only **have** something to say, we have something that you can use.

We want you to use the book, write in it, you may reproduce all or any part or this book for your private use. This book should be used as a **road map** to your future and the betterment of your career. Nothing is more important to you except perhaps your family and your faith.

We will explain the ins and out of putting together a resume, cover letter, interview, how to dress, how to ask questions, the before and after the interview letter, and other related documentation and how to use them as effective job marketing tools.

No time in your life has it been more important to explore your background and experiences. As you go through this book, use the assignments and fill out forms in your best interest. You must not only fill out the forms completely, but it is extremely important that your are totally honest and accurate every step of the way. You have paid for this tool, you owe it to yourself to use it!

What we are going to say now may or may not be the first time you have heard it, but it cannot be said too many times. You must have a battle plan. This is how you are going after the job you want, as they say in marketing, the "Target Market." Who do you want to work for? What kind of a job do you want? In addition to this, and one thing that many job searchers seem to forget, job search is a job, a full-time job. You must make the commitment to put in about 30 hours a week for best result. We have set other parameters for ourselves; some are based upon economics as well as the length of time we can sit in front of a computer. There is outside work too like going to the post office, getting copies made, purchasing materials, as well as interviewing, driving, faxing, and making phone calls. Later in the book, we will review where to get leads, or companies, businesses, and organizations to apply to. It is not as simple as it looks if you are to conduct a campaign. You should put in as much time as you can. Remember, this is the hardest job you will ever have. You must get the right job for you! Use this book to help you at every step along the way.

We cannot tell you what to do. We can suggest and cite personal example as well as compare the methods that may apply. Some of these ideas will work some of the time. To be honest some of them may not. In job search there is no hard and fast rule that states without a shadow of a doubt what will get you an interview and a job every time. All the materials herein is subject to individual evaluation and interpretation.

You must use whatever tactics you feel are right for you when you use them. The situations will vary but the results you want are always the same—"Get the Job." For instance, you will discover we have some goals of our own and know where we want to be. We have selected to send out from 50 to 100 resumes per week to achieve our goal. We spent over $2,000 for job search in 1995. This is a real number, one that we used when we filled out our tax return. On the flip side of this, we have a long-time friend and engineering type who worked for a major aerospace firm who was "downsized" and "outplaced." He would send out maybe 5 or so resumes per week and go fishing. He had few interviews, but at last count, and after being hired at half his wages and again displaced, is back making what he used to and getting overtime too. This was his plan and it worked for him. A recent report from him indicates he is once again out of work after about a year. The choice is yours, but remember, we are sure you have heard it before, "it is a numbers game." The more resumes you send out, the more responses you will receive.

CHAPTER ONE

Getting Started

Hopefully, by the time your have purchased this book or you are reading it, you should have an idea of your career goals. You will have to make a variety of job changes in your career. Across the country, millions of Americans have been forced to change their jobs or vocations. Some by choice, but many more had no choice. Some suggest that we will work no longer than 3-1/2 years per job in would like to think that this is not the rule but the exception. this is apparent. A politician wants to take credit while the sun cause he knows he will be blamed when it rains. The actual time a person spends at a given job appears to be getting shorter. It generally takes from six to eighteen months to train given position. Most people leave the job in two (2) to three This results in a constant turnover of employees. People move sons, but most move (or are moved) because they are not about eighty (80) percent of the people who change jobs. authorities the future. We The reason for is shining be- amount of shorter and a person in a (3) short years. for many rea- happy. This is Many leave because their bosses are not happy with their performance or because they have been laid off work.

The reason we say this is that in the last year, over two million people have been put out of work by "downsizing", "rightsizing", or "pruning". We suggest to you that this will continue to happen everyday, just read the newspaper, listen to the radio or watch the news on TV. Lays offs are everywhere.

This may not be the first thing you want to hear, but we are going to tell you anyway. You, we, all of us need to set some type of goals, career map, or as we call them our A, B, and C plan. You may have to go to D, E, and F, with the economy today. You may have to add more letters of the alphabet. May we suggest that you have many goals to set. You should have short-term, intermediate, and long-term goals.

Transition jobs are the wave of the future. Many of you are becoming "underemployed". This is a term that rarely reaches the media (for good reason). You know who you are out there, but none of our politicians want to touch or mention your group. Transitional jobs will continue forever, but we will see more of them at a faster and faster pace.

More people will be "underemployed" as time goes on. This means they will be underpaid! The employer will pay the least salary possible for any given job.

We don't know if anyone has told you this before, or if you have ever thought of it. The "Plan" concept is somewhat new to us. We didn't stumble on to it until a few years ago when the "Great Recession of 1989" came upon us. A lot of people were thrown out of work when "peace" came. Real peace for the military and aerospace workers meant a long time at the unemployment line. This was the spoils of victors winning of the cold war. That's right. Winning for many engineers, technicians, and high tech workers meant unemployment and/ or underemployment. High-paying jobs were a thing of the past. We remember a long-time colleague of ours who was delighted to get a job at 50 percent of his previous income with a major aerospace company after months and months of job search. He had been with the firm for over fifteen years. Now in his 50s, he has to seek out new employment. He was happy to get a job-any job.

Windows of opportunities open and close all the time, and as we gain maturity, experience, age, or get more education, our plans or goals change, the economy changes. Industries come and go as you know. We have lost many jobs to other countries. Changes is the only thing we can count on. There will be change whether we want it or not. The only question is how we can adjust to it. We must have a plan and goals. For example, you may want to be a sales manager, teacher, architect, doctor, or engineer. Next write it down. You should make a list of your goals and keep it up-to-date. You could carry this out to a needs list. Example, our want list at one time included a "hot" tub, and more. You can carry this out as far as you want. You should have short-term, intermediate, and long-term goals. We also suggest to you to get a small 65 cent notebook and as your needs develop, write them down in the note-book. We suggest that you keep the notebook on you at all times. So as new ideas (goals) come up, you will be prepared to "jot" them down. Modify your list and as you achieve each goal, remove it from your book and add something new. Keep the list as current as you can. As things change revise the list. Put as many goals down as you can identify. Make sure they are in the right order or category. This is not just designed for job search, but for every-thing you want or places you may want to go. This notebook will help you stay on "task" and in the direction you want to go. This simple process could even change your life. We have our own and modify it periodically.

Example:

Income (put a number here)
Position (put a title here)
Part of the country you want to work (put the place here)
Company (put the name of the company you want to work for here)
Vacation (put a place here)
Car (put the kind of car you want)
So forth (put any goal here)

Education (the level you want to achieve or the classes you want to take)
House (the home you want to buy, the price)
Other needs and/or wants

Remember, we want short-term, and intermediate, and long-term goals, items. Make the list long and refer to it on a daily and weekly basis. This will allow you to add, modify subtract items as you achieve them. You will develop a sense of accomplishment as you find yourself making progress by doing this.

The next thing we want to recommend to you is that you develop an attitude of persistence. No matter what, never quit or give up. We hope in your own search that you can do better than this, but don't be discouraged if you don't get action right away when you are sending out your resume. Another piece of information, you will be right on "target" if you get one job offer in ten interviews. We would like to tell you some better things, but this is the national average. Over the past year, we were getting about one interview per 150 resumes. This has not only dropped off, but the quality of companies has also dropped off. This is another area which we want to discuss with you. As a survivor, and depending on your financial situation and goals, the duration of your job search can vary greatly. We want to remind you again, you must not give up and must be consistent. One of the most important things or factors that will make you or your company successful is how consistent your are. What makes advertising successful is consistency and this will work for you. Believe it, if you do what we say, don't give up, continually maintain your efforts, there will be a "payoff". That  potential employer will call you for an interview. There will be times when you get many calls from your efforts, other times no calls at all. It will be feast or famine. Your goals should be around 80 to 100 resumes and/or cover letter mailed out per week. We have developed and also sent out a Newsletter. This is something "new" in job seeking tools that we are experimenting with. We will cover the Newsletter later in another chapter. We will cover every phase of getting the right job.

Let's discuss getting a "stop gap" job. You have to do your search in phases. What do we mean by this? Well, since you know that many positions have been eliminated, a large number of us "downsized", we may be forced to take a position for less money than we are used to making and a position of less authority. This is being under-employed. It may be prudent to look at other industries for this and other employment opportunities. These are not bad moves, they keep money coming in, and may even open up new opportunities for you. We are sure you will be able to develop additional contacts for networking which we have identified as a "key" method of finding that position you really want. The fact is, "Networking" is where 64% to 74% of the jobs come from.

We find that recruitment advertising accounts for 10 to 14 percent, of hiring, and executive search and job agencies account for 9% to 14 percent of hiring. These numbers do not add up to 100%, these numbers change all the time. We would never suggest that you count any of these alternatives down and out. You must keep all options open because you are looking for work. Of course, knowing the statistics will help to keep yourself on track. We will point the way needed to travel to be successful in your job search.

Networking is the "key" method of finding a job. You should be networking at all times. You should tell everyone you see what you do and ask them for help. You may be surprised to get help from unlikely sources like a neighbor who gives you a referral to friend of his. One of our friends got a job referred from his gas station owner who knew a president of a company. You do not know who knows who. Networking is now done cheaply and easily on the internet. The internet is a great way to keep phone bills low and keep in contact with people you know. The more people you know, the more likely it is you will find that special someone who will put you in touch with the hiring manager or give you the idea for your business. Try to keep in contact with people as much as you can. Christmas cards are a good way to do this.

A shift must be made from the traditional sending out of your resumes, which we still do, and we are sure you may have to do. We have discovered, the more effective way of getting the job/position is networking. The power of networking can not be over emphasized.

You may find that "Networking" is challenging for you as it is for us. Given our years of business, marketing, and sales experience we are still learning everyday.

Here is an experience of networking that one of us recently had. Mr. Merhish after being "downsized" from a sales management position without notice. To supplement sending out "cold turkey" job hunting he was sending out around 100 pieces of mail per week, this includes resumes, cover letters, newsletters, and so forth. At that time, he identified three (3) target markets. We will talk about "target marketing" later. He started to call companies to

try to do
this also.
the Industry
that he use
son within
could use a
this "new"
Sometimes it
overturn
reer we are

"cold call" on the phone networking. You can do Mr. Merhish would call businesses that were in that he was in. Some times, he would call people to call on as a salesmen to get the names of per- the firm that might know of an organization that person with his background and training. With name he would continue with this networking. would payoff other time not. But you can not not every rock that is there. Remember it is your ca- talking about.

Networking or cold calls, remember we want to talk to anyone, the guy on the street, the gal at the club or grocery store. By the way, start going to various meetings. We know this is challenging for you to do, is us too. Go to the Rotary Clubs, JC's, Lions Club, Chamber of Commerce, Elk, Masons, Church, or any other or organization in your area to do your networking.

At this moment, if you have no referral names, do not let that stop you. Go to the library find at least two books that will identify businesses in your state or country. Here in California we have the California Manufactures Directory and California Business Directory. We have been told that some libraries have them on the computer. There is also the Robert's Register. You will find similar directors in your library. Talk to your Librarian he/she can help you to identify these reference books. Books are updated yearly.

Mr. Merhish has the California Manufactures Directory on his computer and he uses it all the time. There is also The Thomas Director listing national companies. Business Directories are very useful. The directories have the name of the offices, size of company, what they do or sell, officer in the company etc. If you are interested in buying this directory, be prepared to put out more than $800.00. The library is a very cost effective resource.

You can identify the companies by there SIC codes (this is the code that identifies what they do). It will give you city, product, and so forth. Next, select the company to be contacted. For us, we identify companies from 5 to 30 million gross sales per year. This is where we see ourselves most valuable and the greatest opportunities for us. Since we have the name of the company the phone number, and its president "Voila" we can call, write, fax, or E-mail them.

No matter how you come up with a name, it is important to develop a "script". This is especially true if you're calling. We would suggest to you that you want to sound professional and to the point. These people that you are calling are very busy, and you will need to get the point across quickly and to hold their attention. You will also run up against the "gate keeper". This is usually the secretary of the person your are trying to contact. Since in most cases the person you want to talk to is the president of the company or director of the firm, the "gatekeeper" is the first one we have to sell.

Here are some calls Mr. Merhish had made doing cold call "Networking. The first one, he called was to the president of a medium sized firm. Having years of experience in the Compressed air industry he was known by his reputation in the field and got right in. He told the president that he wasn't looking for a job with this firm, but he was looking to network, and he ask the gentleman if he knew of anyone he could talk to. Mr. Merhish suggested that he was "downsized" from his position as sales and marketing manager. The president told him that he didn't know anyone he could talk to. Mr. Merhish left his name and of course his phone number. It was hoped that he would call. Do not try to second guess or overlook any opportunity.

Now Mr. Merhish is "hot", right? That went pretty well. He was ready for a larger firm. Mr. Merhish is ready to call another firm and another president. Sure enough he gets the "gate keeper". This is going to challenge for him he thought and it did. He got the third degree from the gatekeeper who was the secretary to the president. Mr. Merhish assures the gate keeper that he is not looking for a job, just wants to network with the president. We must tell you that the "gate keeper" was empathic, but she was not going to let Mr. Merhish

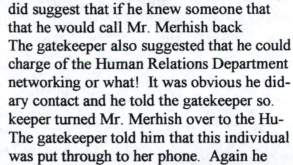

talk to her boss. She knew the president (Networking right?). talk to the person in (HR). Hey! Is this n't know an intermedi- At this point the gate- man Resource person. was very good, and he did suggest that if he knew someone that that he would call Mr. Merhish back The gatekeeper also suggested that he could charge of the Human Relations Department networking or what! It was obvious he did- ary contact and he told the gatekeeper so. keeper turned Mr. Merhish over to the Human The gatekeeper told him that this individual was put through to her phone. Again he told his tale, this time the HR person told him that this was a hard way to network and that he should get and work with a "headhunter". They discussed this option. She also told him that he could send his resume and newsletter in for review. At this point he asked if he would mind critiquing his submittals and get back to him. She agreed to this. He felt that this was a good way to see how his stuff looked. They ended the conversation. However, about a week later, the Human Relation person left a message on his answering service, she had reviewed Mr. Merhish's cover letter, newsletter, and resume.

Networking is "critical" to your success in job searching. Always remain on good terms with former bosses. This may or may not be easy, however, they may have referrals to other areas of employment when you are "downsized" out the door. Do not "panic" when you get "downsize". It is not the end of the world. Try to leave on good terms with your old employer. Complete all of your projects and let your boss know how hard you worked. There are good reasons for this. They may like you but cannot afford to keep you. Ask for a severance package. Some companies have severance packages, most do not.

Companies give severance packages to avoid bitterness and lawsuits especially for good employees who may be due things like bonuses. Always ask for a letters of recommendation. This will make it harder for the employer to say you were downsized because you were a bad worker. You would have their work in writing as to what happened. Employers feel the need to justify why they let you go. Ask for an explanation as to why you were laid off. This will help you to explain it to future employers. Be sure you tell the new employer what happened. Ask if the employers know of any openings in your company or any other companies or industries. Always go to the top of the company to get leads. You do not know who will help you. Know your company policy regarding laying off workers. Find out if there is any possibility of recall by the company. Always get and read the personnel manual and be sure that the company follows manual guidelines. Many times the companies fail to follow all the procedures required before you are laid off. You will never get any due process once you are gone. You will be out of sight and out of mind. They will quickly forget everything about you while they try to figure out who will get stuck with your work. Someone will get stuck with it! The work does not go away

Ask for typing assistance on your resume and letter of introduction. See if you can use the company's phone, office, stationery, copier or desk to set up interviews with other firms. Also see if you can get time off with pay for interviewing. Finally, ask your employer if there is any other help they may want to give you like outplacement services. Outplacement

service is going to an outside organization specializing in placement of workers who have been downsized. Usually there is no cost to you. The cost is picked up by the employer. However, in some situations, you may have to pay for your own outplacement work. Ask about any benefits or 401K funds you may be due. Find out when you last day at your current job will be.

Some companies will give you a check you and not require your to come to work. Ask about continuing your health benefits. COBRA is a good possibility if you need it.

We are our most important product. Market yourself well. We are a commodity that must compete to get that next job. This may be a "new" concept for you non-marketing and sales types, but the sooner you recognize the fact that you are the most important product you have, the sooner you will understand the task before you. Do not forget for a minute, there are lots of applicants out there for every job. It has been estimated each job will have from twenty to 300 applicants. This may sound hard to believe, but it is true, even in a good economy with low employment rates.

The authors are aware of a Regional Managers position that was available with the Staples organization. They are a national retailing outlet. In conversations with them, the authors learned that they had eighty (80) applicants for one position. This seems to be more the rule than the exceptions these days. The numbers can be much higher for better jobs. The better the job, the more people will apply. The more the job is publicized, the more people will apply. A recent position that was advertised in the paper had 1,000 openings of which 300 would be females, however it was reported that over 3,000 people applied for these jobs! Clearly, there were three (3) applicants for every position. Do not be disappointed if you fail to get a job like this. The jobs are there but you have to keep trying. You will have to literally turn over every stone until you find the job or position your really want.

Sometimes you can get a lucky break and just walk into a great job. This is not true most of the time. You will really have to look to find your ideal jobs. The job will never just find you.

CHAPTER TWO

Supply and Demand

You should attempt to understand the basic laws of supply and demand. Supply and demand are the "**key**" things in any economy. The more supply of any given commodity, the less the demand there is for it. There is no demand at all for things when in infinite supply. Therefore, if you are highly skilled and there is a need for many person with your skill you are in a positive position. But if there are many people with your skills the chance for future employment becomes difficult.

You are a commodity. You **must** go out and sell your services to the highest bidder you can find. You are in constant competition with all the other people with your same level of skills.

The market will give you a "**fair**" price for your services. Most people feel that they are worth more than they are getting. You are not alone if you feel this.

A recent newspaper article stated that the average college graduate expects to receive a salary of $38,000 per year. This optimistic view is somewhat unrealistically high for most graduates. As an example, the starting salaries for college graduate and full credential teacher have an average in California of $30,000 per year (in 1997). Furthermore, it is projected that by 2005 almost half of the jobs in American will require that over 50% of the workers have training in information technology. Therefore, if the applicant does not have this training and background he will be in a position to not be hired at all. The fastest-growing occupations will require the most education and concentration in business- services and health-services industries.

Many industries are going to a two-tiered wage system. This means older workers continue to get their higher salary and benefits. New workers are brought in at much lower wages. The new employees will receive about 1/3 the wage of the higher-paid, older employee for the same work. This trend is likely to continue as companies seek to drive costs down. This results in less expensive products and more sales for the firm. The company gains greater profits and higher bonuses for the top people. This is done in the name of competition and efficiency. The supposed shortage of skilled employees can be ignored by the company as long as persons apply to take these entry level openings.

The company believes that the older, higher-priced employees will train the new, lesser-paid employees as long as their pay and benefits are not reduced. This strategy seems to be working especially in view of few labor strikes or work stoppages. The reason for this is "downsizing". There are few labor unions to represent the workers; in fact, the percentage of workers represented by unions has dropped to an all-time low. The companies are not satisfied at leaving this situation alone. They offer the older employees a "Golden Hand Shake" (retirement offer) once the new employees have been trained. The worker either takes the golden hand shake or does not. The company has eliminated the older employee if he accepts the golden handshake. The company may lay off the employee the following year if he does not accept the retirement offer. Either way, the company wins! Now the worker will be out of a job whether or not he takes the golden hand shake or not. The older worker might be offered his old position back within a year but at the new lower wage. Generally, the worker is better off taking the golden hand shake and looking for new employment elsewhere. The older worker will soon be looking for work with or without the golden hand shake.

The companies are justified in laying off older employees who refuse to take the golden hand shake for purely economic reason. This has been upheld by some state Supreme Courts. The older worker has no recourse against the company once it has been refused. The company may lay off the employees. Lastly, there may not be a golden hand shake at all. The cards are all stacked in favor of the companies at this point.

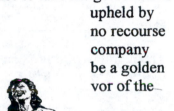

It is true that in some work environments, there are genuine labor shortages. If you have these job skills, you find a large demand for what you have to offer. But if this is the case, you are going to find more people attracted to your type of job which means greater competition, decreasing, salaries, and the possibility of being "downsized" when ripples occur in the economy.

You can increase your "value" by getting extra training, more education, or obtaining additional work experience. You should always be looking for ways to improve your "value." There are areas with a limited supply or workers and hence a high salary. Great professional basketball players can demand and get a very good salary. On the other hand, the trained "fireman" on a train will get a fairly low salary because there is no demand for their services in the age of the modern trains. The fact is, there are no firemen modern trains.

You can determine what your value is to the market by just looking at what you are making. You may like your job and decide to keep it. The value of your job is not determined solely by you but rather by the market. The market is not personal.

The market determines value by supply and demand. The more the supply, the less the demand and vice versa. Every person has at least some value to the market. If nothing else, as a consumer of products. The number of jobs created outside the farm sector far exceeds the forecast of 233,000 per year by private economists. So if you have the right experience, there should be a slot for your out there. If not you owe it to yourself to develop salable skills that meets the needs of the demand.

Any material object has value to someone. *"One man's trash is another man's treasure."* You need to develop talents into marketable skills that can be sold to the highest bidder.

You must first know what you have to sell. This workbook will show you how to inventory you skills to help you to make that import determination.

Remember that supply and demand control almost everything in the economy. Supply and demand apply to you and your organization. Supply and demand are everywhere. 1.1 million new, good jobs were created in the past year.

You need to find your "niche" where you can be happy, but at the same time, make as much money as possible to meet your needs. There are trade-offs here and you must understand them. It has been discovered that all people have one thing in common. diverse personalities and traits but they great deal of time at work. You must if you want to go to the top. Most put time for their firms. In the beginning, will not be compensated. At some ganization naturally rewards this loy-promotions and pay raises. This trans-spending less time with your family. may not want to pay this price. Your more important to you. This is your call. 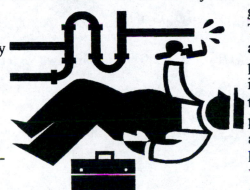 great business They have very all spend a put in the hours in a lot of over-this overtime point, the or-alty with more lates into You may or family may be

Most Leaders in any organization put in at least 50 to 60 hours a week at work. A manager will be replaced by a less capable person who is more willing to put in the hours. If he starts to cut back on his hours. This is generally fatal to a career, however in some cases, people can figures out how to use the time best to make even more money for the organization. These people can actually cut back on hours they work on the job but make more money for the firm. This is by far the best use of time and experience. This is a good for them and better for the company. It is a win win situation for all.

Everyone from the richest man in the world to the poorest man in the world has at least one thing in common. They all have exactly 24 hours in a day, seven days in a week and

This is only a partial list, so your list may be much longer than ours and will vary with your own back grounds.

List Everything you Have:

You will want to make sure that you recognize your computer skills and any foreign language. You will want to list the language and the appropriate skill and levels.

Example:

IBM   B3900 HP   Fortran IV   Dell   Gateway   Photoshop 5.5 INS/DLI

GEM   Illustrator 8.0 PageMaker 6.5 plus   Acrobat 4.0   Office 2000   S10000/3000

Mark IV   ADF   ACT 2.0   Windows 98   Power Point   Publisher   Basic

Lotus 1-2-3   Windows 95 Windows 2000   WordStar   Word Perfect-Compaq

QuickBooks   JAVA IMP   Compatibles   CD-Rewriterable   Windows NT 4.0

Pascal

You should identify degrees, certificates, special course work, seminars, and workshops. In addition, list all skills, tools, machine knowledge, licenses, hobbies, interests, clubs, and Positions held. All of us have notable information that could be valuable, such things as Awards, books, articles, papers, and so forth.

Marketable Facts & Notable Information

Sometime in the game of job search and interviewing is the question of what are your preerences. At this time, I want you to identify you choices.

Location (List your choices in each category in order of preference:

	State	County
City:		
1st Choice		
2nd Choice		
3rd Choice		
4th Choice		

Position Words

To help you have a better understanding of your primary background and experience, we would like you to circle each word that most closely describes these areas:

Operations Management

Senior Management

Sales

Computer Applications

Management

Sales Management

Senior Executive

Junior Executive

Manufacturing Engineering

Organizational Management

Management

Retail Management

Engineering

Program Management

Production Management

Educational Management

Teacher

Marketing Management

Training Management

Technical Applications

Engineering

Any Other Areas you May Have Experience In

Position Words II

Here are some additional position words that may describe your overall accomplishment, duties, experiences, and background. Circle each word that correctly covers these areas:

Marketing	Import	Export
Financial	Projects	Media
MIS	Design	Promotions
Operations	Proposals	Project Management
Analysis	Public Relations	Employee Development
Start-up	Financial Operation	Project
Administration	Reorganizing	Account Retention
Training & Development	Organization	Electronics
International Relations	Purchasing	Liaison
Business Development	Account Executive	Manufacturing
Information Systems	Production Control	Administrative
Product Introduction	Customer Service	Programming
Government Requirement	Process Planning	Product Engineering
Computer Application	Sales	Sales Training
Franchise Operations	Negotiations	User Interface
Expansion Planning		

Position Statements

Complete the following statements by checking all appropriate answers and filling in the requested information.

1. My experience and background can best be described as (choose all that apply):

extensive	management
solid	progressive
well-rounded	hands-on
broad	in-depth
technical	comprehensive
senior level	diversified

Any other experiences you have.

Complete these sentences utilizing the above words which will assist you to focus your background experience.

1. _____.

2. _____.

3. _____.

2. My experience, background and accomplishments have been developed within or through the following types of environment (check all that apply):

Fast-paced	Highly competitive	results oriented
Volatile	technical	marketing/sales
Operations	creative	engineering
Practical training	international	profit-oriented
Government	state-of-the-art	diversified
Financial	education	flexible
ever-changing	high-stress	management
Consulting	service-oriented	deadline sensitive
Successful	top secret	analytical
Sales intensive	research	profitable

3. My experience, background and accomplishments are further demonstrated through (check all that apply and fill in information when necessary):

a results oriented track record   revenue enhancement

worldwide exposure   problem solving challenges

exposure to complex situations   profitable accomplishments

continuous formal education   project development

exposure to European markets   International background

rapid advancement   go the extra mile

progressive growth and accomplishments

Full responsibility for:_____.

Course work in:_____.

Direct interface with:_____.

Innovative design of:_____.

Production of :_____.

An education background in: _____.

In-depth knowledge of: _____.

Job Functions

1. Place a dash (-) in front of each function you have experienced (business or personal).

2. Place a (+) in front of each function for which you would like to be responsible in your next job.

3. Place a double plus (++) in front of the functions you want to be involved with on a hands-on/day-to-day basis. Indicate a minimum of 3 but no more than five.

Accounting	Plant Management	Engineering
Administration	Pharmaceutical	Environmental
Advertising	Public relations	Executive
Agriculture	Personnel	Electronics
Artist	Planning	Field Service
Auditor	Pricing	Financial Analyst
Aviation	Product Design	Food service
Automotive	Production Engineering	Financial
Adjuster	Project Engineering	Banking
Psychology	Government	Health Recreation
Broker	Publishing	Graphics
Budget	Buyer	Quality Control
Chemical Engineering	Human Resources	Civil Engineering

Health Care	Recruiting	Clergy
Research & Development	Industrial Engineer	Commercial Banking
Retailing	Communication	Insurance
Sales	Community Service	Security
Computer Programmer	International	Consultant
Investment Counseling	Scientific Consultant Law	Surveyor
System Analyst	Contract Administrator	Copywriter
Labor Relations	Structural Engineering	Management
Costing	Software Systems	Marketing
Credit/collection	Manufacturing	Construction
Social Science	Ceramic	Technical
Mass Communications	Control	Material
Traffic & Shipping	Data Processing	Mechanical Eng.

Design & Drafting	Medical	Urban Development
Development engineer	Military	Metallurgy
Distribution	Merchandising	New Products
Editing	Natural resources	Operations
Energy	Other_____	Other_____

Additional Areas in which you may have been involved: _____
_____.

In summary of this exercise, you have now identified the areas in which you have experience, areas in which you would like to have more experience and responsibility and the three to five areas which you would like to have hands on responsibility for on a day to day basis.

When writing your resume use al of the words from this exercise that accurately describes your job functions.

QUESTIONS

Here is a list of questions and concerns which every employer would like to discover about every applicant. We can not tell you that you will be asked every one of these questions in a single interview, but we can state that you will be asked many of them. We suggest that you prepare yourself by answering every question herein and review your answers many times so that when you are in an interview setting, you will be able to recall your response.

1. HONESTY

Rarely is an interviewer going to ask you, "Are you honest" so somehow you are going to have to assure him that you are.

You may provide letters which indicate you can be trusted or make a statement to that effect.

On the lines below, write a statement you feel comfortable with that would address this and assure the employer of your honesty.

_____

_____

_____

_____

_____

2. RESPONSIBILITY

All employers want to know that you are the type of person who is going to be on the job every day and on time.

He will also want to know that when given a job to do you will get it done and done correctly.

On the lines below, develop a statement that will indicate to the employer you are a responsible person.

_____

_____

_____

3. CHARACTER

An employer is always seeking to discover character flaws or weaknesses.

You will want to get across that you are not perfect but that you are constantly working on self improvement.

On the lines below, write a statement that would best describe how you feel if you were asked.

_____

_____

_____

_____

4. PROBLEM SOLVER

An employer us always looking for employees that can solve problems, not create them. In doing this the employer may ask you perhaps the most difficult question of all to answer. The question, "Why should we hire you?"

On the lines below write out a statement that you are comfortable with which indicates that you are in fact, a problem solver and why you are the correct person for the job.

_____

_____

_____

_____

5. FOLLOWS DIRECTIONS

Every employer is looking for people who can follow directions. Therefore, it is a good idea that you convey to the employer that you are a creative person, yet you believe that it is important to work within company procedures and regulations.

On the following lines write a statement that will indicate to the employer that you can follow directions and procedures.

_____

_____

_____

_____

6. PUTS COMPANY BUSINESS FIRST

Employers are always looking for employees who are interested in the growth and development of their business.

The applicant that projects a more positive image with regard to interest un the quality of the product, service, or the profit of the company will stand a better chance of getting the position that he/she is interviewing fir,

The self-centered individual who takes little interest in the growth of the company or wastes valuable time or resources would be the last kind of employee the company would want as an employee.

On the lines below, write a statement that you feel good about that would show the employer that you would indeed be an asset to their firm.

_____

_____

_____.

7. HEALTHY EMPLOYEE

With rising cost of health care, the employer has a great concern with health care issues and problems. There is a heavy cost to an employer when employees miss work frequently.

If you are in good health, when asked, simply state, "I am in great health and I will be at work everyday. You may want to stress attendance at your previous place of employment or your school attendance if it was good.

If you have letters, certificates, anything that relates to your health, efficiency or punctuality, bring them.

You will want to point that you have a strong sense of self-discipline and that any ailment might have will not affect your work or attendance.

On the lines below, develop your own statement which you can use when asked about your health.

_____

_____

_____.

8. ENTHUSIASM

An enthusiastic employee will be welcomed. The employer recognizes the value of a contented work environment. It is realized that one negative employee can cause disputes, cliques, scandal, malice, jealousy and more.

The employer is looking for a person that can get along, one with charisma and a good sense of humor. This type of person will get the job over someone who can not break into a smile.

You need to be warm, friendly, relaxed, above all be yourself. Smile and laugh at the interviewers jokes (be real).

Bear in mind, to get the job, the interviewer must like you. The more he/she likes you, the less emphasis will be placed on your resume and qualifications.

The interviewer will ask you questions about your personality. On the lines below write some short statements, one-liners that you can use in your interview as the opportunity comes up.

_____

_____

_____

_____

9. WHY DO YOU WANT TO WORK HERE?

We can not tell you how many times we have been asked, "Why do you want to work here?" If you have done your research and goal setting, you will be in a position to answer this question in a positive manner.

An important tip: You want to sound sincere and not 'canned'. You may want to suggest that you see the company as a place where you can make your mark, make a contribution and be successful. You can suggest here that you feel well qualified to be an asset to the firm.

On the lines below, write your own statement as to why you want to work for this company.

_____

_____

_____

_____

10. CHANGE IN CAREER

This question you may find a but challenging, but you can be assured that a potential employer is going to ask it of you if you are in fact making a career change. You may suggest that this was something you have been training for a long time. or that you have, because self-examination and research, decided to look at career options that could be better and more productive for your future.

Now take your time, but in your own words, develop a statement that best presents your reason for making a career change, if this is what you are doing.

_____

_____

_____

11. WHY WERE YOU OUT OF WORK FOR SUCH A LONG TIME?

If there is any question that we have some experience with, this is one that we know. We assure you that when you are in front of the interviewer, this question will be asked and it will be hard to answer. It is not, in many cases today, your fault. Many of us have been 'downsized.' Nevertheless, it is up to us to come up with an answer that is acceptable in the eyes of the potential employer. Be honest. Any tale that you might weave can come back to harm you in the future. It may be painful; we have a few painful tales in our past, most of us do. The Bible says, "The Truth Will Set You Free." We believe this will be true when you discuss your work history.

Do not dwell on anything or place blame. You may discuss time in self-examination not wanting to rush into another dead-end job. Of course discuss tune in researching companies that you would like to work for.

Now on the lines below, write your own statement.

_____

_____

_____

12. THE JOB HOPPER

The question of job hopping may or may not come up in your interview, but it has in ours. We have been employed with several companies that could not make payroll or have gone out of business. If you have had this experience we can assure you that you will be asked this question. Again, be honest and be brief.

You may of course, discuss the fact that you got smart and analyzed your job skills and desires as well as researched potential employers in order to pursue a life-long career.

You can tell the interviewer that you have in the past, just taken the first job that comes along, if this is truly the case.

You can make the statement that your job hopping days are over. However, we we would suggest that you avoid any reference to 'Job Hopping' if you can. The less said of this the better.

In your own words, discuss why, if this is the case, you were a 'Job Hopper.' You may want to avoid using the words 'Job Hopper.' Given the trend to restructure, downsize, and rightsize many persons have found themselves in this situation

_____

_____

_____

13. SUPERVISORY EXPERIENCE

The employer is always on the lookout for individuals with management and supervisory experience. If you have little, draw from your personal experience with groups and organizations. You may have experience in clubs, church, or sport groups. If so, state it.

If you have direct business management or supervisory experience, you will want to inform the interviewer.

In your own words write down the answer about your management or supervisory experience.

_____

_____

_____

14. REVIEW THE LAST INTERVIEW

This will be a valuable exercise and will be a powerful tool on your next job interview. Write down all of the questions that you were asked during your last interview. Believe it or not, the more you interview the more powerful and better applicant you will be.

It is essential that you write down the questions that were most difficult for you. Prepare answers for these questions.

_____

_____

_____

_____

_____

15. ANY OTHER INFORMATION NOT ALREADY MENTIONED

_____

_____

_____

_____

_____

AFTERTHOUGHT

Think before answering any questions. Why is this question being asked? Try to understand what the interviewer is trying to disclose. Answers can often reveal things about you that are better left unstated.

WHAT EMPLOYERS CAN NOT ASK YOU

Today, the laws are very clear as to what specifically an employer or interviewer can ask an applicant. The following are questions you do not have to answer. However, let us point out that not answering the question may lead to not getting a job. We are totally aware of labor laws, but ask yourself these questions: Do you want the job; Do you have the time to go to court; how valuable is keeping the information confidential? Here is our point-you be the judge. We are only going to point out what they can not ask. We can recall one interview where the General Manager asked, "How long are you going to work before you retire?" Clearly an illegal question, but the job was not only wanted but needed. The answer was given in a positive way, one that would sell the applicant and suggested there would be many years of employment before retirement.

It is illegal to ask the following of you:

1. Your sex, marital status, if you are divorced or separated, when a divorce would be final if you live with anyone, etc.

2. If you have children, how many, how old, who cares for them, if you are planning on more children, whether or not the children live with you.

3. Physical information such as height, weight, physical/mental handicaps, etc. unless the job has specific health requirements.

4. If you have ever been arrested, jailed, or convicted of a crime (unless a security clearance is a requirement for the job).

5. If you have military background, which branch of the service you were in; if you received an honorable discharge.

6. Any reference to age other than, "Are you over 18?"

7. If you own a home, rent, etc.

8. Any questions pertaining to your religious beliefs.

RESPONSES TO ILLEGALQUESTIONS

As we suggested on the previous pages, you must use your common sense when dealing with illegal questions.

* If you believe that the interviewer has not motive other than finding the best applicant, and you do not feel an honest answer can cause you difficulty in being employed, go ahead and answer the question. Ignore the fact that this is an illegal question.

* If you are concerned that an honest answer could knock you out of the running for a position, try to tactfully turn the situation around and as the interviewer, "How is this information important in selecting a new employee?" You could suggest to the interviewer that you have never been asked that question. It is not a good idea simply remind the interviewer that the question is not legal.

* Telling someone that "you are wrong," especially the interviewer can be very costly for you. It could cost you the job. Finding out why the question was asked may not be worth the consequences, and you may as well answer the question.

* If you find that the interviewer is persistent in asking illegal questions and it is obviously unreasonable, then you might state, "I do not believe that these questions are relevant to the requirements of the position for which I am interviewing." Remember, this could cost you the position, but you may be better off not working for this company or organization.

RESEARCH   RESEARCH   RESEARCH

Before we go off and write that 'glowing' and meaningful cover letter and resume, we recommend that you take some time to find out about the potential employers that you are thinking of working for. We suggest that you take some time to check them out. This is a more intelligent way of selling yourself. In addition, it is the only way that you will learn the procedures, policies, and attitudes of the prospective employer. Simply stated, if you do not do this you will be essentially whistling in the wind. This is your future you are dealing with so you be the judge as to what a little research is worth.

By answering the following question you will have a significant advantage in developing a winning cover letter and resume

> Do you have sufficient feelings for the employer to make an intelligent decision as to whether or not you would want to go to work for them?

If after research you have decided that this is not the employer for you, you will not have to waste your time developing applicant materials. You now have saved yourself time to devote to other potential employers. Not only have you saved postage but perhaps time wasted working for an undesirable employer.

On the lines below indicate what you have discovered about each employer you research. Indicate who you would work for, who the interviewer might be, problems within the company, particular problems related to the job you are looking at, company contacts and any other important information you have learned.

Employer:_____

_____

Employer:_____

_____ >

Employer:_____

_____

By completing this exercise you have discovered many of the things a 'headhunter' would learn from the same exercise. You may have discovered that the person or persons who will be making the final hiring decision is not the person conducting the interview.

Do you have the facts, figures, information about the size of the firm, annual sales, officers of the corporation, industry, plans for future growth, policies, procedures, profitability, position in the marketplace, competitors, etc? Every one of these items will have an effect on your future if you take a position with the firm. On the lines below write down those items which have influenced you to make a decision about the companies you have researched.

Company:_____

_____.

Company:_____

_____.

Company:_____

_____.

Job descriptions are very important. If a firm or organization is in the process of hiring this information is usually published. However, it can be a verbal description. The job description is invaluable as it will provide you with specific information which can be used to customize your resume and cover letter point by point. Government agencies (state & federal) as well as school systems routinely print their job descriptions. This information is available at your local employment office.

Private sector information is of course available from each potential employer. This information may be more difficult to obtain and will vary from employer to employer. However, Private sector job descriptions are often posted within the employment offices of the employer and may also be posted with private job search firms.

On the lines below write down job descriptions for those companies you are interested in.

1._____.

2._____.

Chapter Eight

Sources for Jobs

There are a great many sources for jobs. We will try to discuss some of them here with you in this workbook. We have suggested that over 80 percent of the jobs are gotten by the technique of networking. But you should not rely on only one source. This section will not be in priority, but it will suggest areas and how they may work for you.

The first thing that comes to mind, one that you may have used in the past, is the National Job Newspaper published by The Wall Street Journal. The cost for this tabloid is around $36.00, so it is a little pricey in our pinion, but if it works for you, then it is worth the investment. The paper covers jobs nationally, so a decision has be made if you are willing to relocate. You should not restrict yourself, but this needs to be an decision you will have to make. This tabloid is much like a the newspaper Help Wanted Section of your local newspaper. It will generate many applicants for few positions. Yes, the jobs in this document are upscale, but are the tabloid is reaching many people seeking employment from all parts of the country. You will have to realize that this paper has a circulation of thousands of job hunters. The tabloid does have tips on job search and other timely and valuable material, so you my find it a valuable investment.

You may use the local newspaper, the Los Angeles Times, Orange County Register, New York Times, Press Enterprise, Long Beach Press, Des Moines Tribune, or what other major paper that may be circulated in your community. These papers bring not only local national and some international position. can count on having many competitors for position you might apply for. You may be a man, accountant, Engineer, or manager. are going to want to apply for the position looking for your skills. But what if you are sales manager and you answered an ad placed for an Engineer? No you are not applying for the Engineer position, you are going apply for a Marketing Management job. Is it is open, we don't know. Here is what this approach will do for you. First, your are applying for a position that is not being advertised. Therefore automatically we have eliminated over 60 to 100 applicants. That's right, you have a chance to be "Johnny on the spot" or maybe not. You are also going answer the ads for your experience and job title, and so is everyone else.

but You each sales- You that a

Which is better? Neither. The best one is the one that get you the job.

Most industrial magazines have a job search section in the back. Most of these are limited, but they are there. These jobs are much like the ones in the newspaper in that you find they are open to everyone and anyone to apply for. A stone that should not go unturned. You will want to find directed toward industries and products. You will find magazines published by nearly every product, association, and industry.

At your local University, or Public Library, you should find many sources for job search. There is the Thomas Guide, Business and Manufactures directories. We have the California Manufactures Director on our computer. This directory has around 36,000 manufactures in it. This directory on disk may be purchased for around $800.00. The books are much less and using the library is of course "free." With the aid of the Manufactures Directory, you can identify the size of the company, what they make, officers' names, address, phone numbers, a lot of history that assists in determining if this is the kind of company you would like to be associated with. However, It doesn't tell us the personality of the company or business orientation, attitude, but neither does the newspaper. It is a fact that it is very difficult to get attitude or business orientation. This is an important issure and will or could determine if this is the company you would really like to work for.

If you are in sales and marketing, most likely you would want to work for a firm that favors the importance of this area. It is not as simple as it seems. Some companies believe that marketing and sales are the most important elements within the firm. Others may lean another way, that sales and marketing are a necessary evil but not to take seriously. You can ask, if given a chance, are you a production-oriented or marketing-oriented firm? Does the company have a business plan. marketing plan, of 3 or 5 year plan, what is their goals? We will deal with more these questions later.

Some companies are run by the engineering and for engineers. A company is aerospace may be like this. You should plan to go to night school to get an engineering degree if you get a job at a company like this. You will not advance without an engineering degree in this type of company.

If you don't know by now, more than 80 percent of the jobs are gotten though networking. You may not have the luxury of totally networking. You should be networking at all the time. Spend some money and buy yourself some business cards. You should hand out two types of business cards-one that represents the firm you are with and the other that presents you. You can also carry around some blank cards. But which is more professional is up to you.

Another source which is "free" is your Business to Business, or Yellow-paged phone book. This resource will have just about every company that is in business in your area or region that you would like to work for . What these directories can't do for you is to give you the size of the organization or the name of the important contact, or owner within the business. You can add this source to your inventory of potential employers, and you will have a large inventory of companies to choose from.

You don't want to forget the Wall Street journal itself as a source of employment. We don't know anyone that has gotten a job out of this media, but this is not to say that people don't. Depending on the degree of your pursuit, you can get every major newspaper in the country. We have found that most of these papers can be located at major bookstores and in your nearest library.

There are also local tabloids, as an example, Orange County has a business newspaper where every week besides business news, they "showcase" a number of businesses. They identify the president, size of the firm, what they do, address, and the phone number. The reason we like this medium is that you are getting a good source with a key contact person identified and limited competition for employment. Some of companies may not be in the field of your expertise, but the cost of the resource is right. It is "free". Look in your area for such a business tabloid.

Two other areas or references that may be overlooked by many is the Health Care Reference Source & Buyers Guide and the Directory of Manufacturer's Sales Agencies. The Health Care Reference has companies and service in the Health Care Industry. You may get this source from Medi-Pages, Inc. 757 Cayuga Street Lewiston, New York 14092. Their phone number is 1-800-554-6661. You will give another place to look up companies to apply to. The Directory of Manufacturer's Sales Agents could offer a complete new source of places to send your resume to. This book has independent sales and marketing companies that from time to time are looking for people to bring into their organizations to help expand their marketing and sales. The benefit to you is this is generally an unknown area of job opportunities. You can contact the Association of Manufacturers Agents at P.O. Box 3467 Laguna Hills, California 92654. The book sell in the $30.00 range.

Another "new" source is the "net,", Internet, or the "Web." Whatever you want to call it, it seems that there are many companies looking for qualified applicants who have internet experience, or at least know how to move around the internet. It is suggested that these jobs pay from $30,000 to $200,000. This calls special experience, but here is a place to look and put your resume. You must remember however, that when the call goes out for jobs on the web, that often this call is world wide in scope and that these job vacancies are reaching thousands of applicants.

The net can be used both offensively and defensively.

The net is used offensively when you put your resume out on the various web sites. This has the advantage of being able to get your resume out on the various web sites. This has the advantage of being able to get your resume out to a lot of companies. The disadvantage is that your company may see your resume on the web and lay you off. One applicant was laid off after his boss 'discovered' the applicant's resume on the 'web.' The boss told him that he might be more comfortable looking for a job full time.

The web can also be used defensively by going out to various web sites and seeing what jobs are there. You will be able to see what the company is about so that you can decide if you want to send them your resume or not. The major disadvantage to this method is that it takes a lot of time. Time is one thing that most job seekers do not have a lot of.

If you are running out of places to send your resume, you can contact one of the mailing list firms, like the Mailing List of Southern California, 1-800-352-7450. This company can provide you will thousands of company names and addresses.

INFORMATION SOURCES FOR MAJOR EMPLOYERS

If you are considering relocating for employment opportunities you will find the Chamber of Commerce a great source of information about potential employers. Request that the Chamber of Commerce send you a membership catalog.

Do not overlook the libraries. Go to your public or University library and talk with the head librarian or the business reference librarian. The librarians job is to help people and they do enjoy finding solutions. The following list of directories and references can be found at your community library or University library in your area.

The Fortune Directory of U.S. Corporations

Published by Fortune Directories, 229 West 28th Street, New York, NY 10001
Prepaid copies for $10.00
This directory includes the Fortune 500 list of the largest industrial companies and the Fortune Service 500 list of top non-industrials. The lists can only help you with standings within these top 500 companies. Corporate names and addresses are not available.

Moody's Industrial Manual

Published by Moody's Investor Service (A subsidiary of Dunn & Bradstreet)
99 Church Street, New York, NY 10007; Phone 212-553-0300
This manual is a good source of financial and business information on every indus trial company listed on the New York Stock Exchange and over 500 companies listed on regional exchanges. The manual will provide a history of these companies and information on their subsidiaries, affiliates, products and services, principle plants, management, and names of officers and directors. You will find this manual to be a very good resource in your j ob search.

International Directory of Corporate Affiliations

Published by The National Register Publishing Company
3004 Glenview Road, Wilmette, IL 60091
This directory lists foreign companies with U.S. holdings and 1,400 U.S. corpora
tions which have overseas affiliates, subsidiaries, and divisions. This will be helpful
if you are looking for employment in a foreign country. You will also find the complete names and addresses of 95 consulates in the United States.

Directory of Leading Private Companies

Published by the National Register Publishing Company
3004 Glenview Road, Wilmette, IL 60091
This is a unique directory in that it lists invaluable information about this country's
top 3500 privately owned corporations You will find names and title of key contacts
number of subsidiaries, number of employees, assets, liabilities, net worth, types of
computer hardware, addresses and phone numbers.

American Society of Training and Development Directory

Published by the Association of the same name
6000 Maryland Avenue, Suite 305, S.W., Washington, D.C. 20024
This directory covers "Who's Who in Training and Development" throughout
the United States.

Thomas Register of American Manufacturers

Published by Thomas Publishing Co.
1 Penn Plaza, New York, NY 10007
You will find this at your local library. The register contains information about
thousands of businesses, large and small in just about every field. This is a twelve
volume set if books. The books contain names, locations, phone numbers, and the
products that each company is manufacturing and marketing.

Standard and Poor's Register of Corporations, Directors and Executives

Published by McGraw Hill, New York, NY 10007
This is a three volume set of books. The first volume lists all of the major compa
nies by industry and geographic location. The second volume gives details and

Contract information on these companies, and the third volume represents personal data n many corporate executives.

Dunn's Employment Opportunity Directory/The Career Guide

Published by Dunn & Bradstreet, New York, NY 10007
This is an excellent guide for the job seeker as it lists over 4,000 companies and names, titles, addresses and phone numbers. It also provides a projection of career opportunities within each company and the educational specialties each company hires.

The National Job Bank

Published by Bob Adams, Inc,
840 Summer Street, Boston, MA 02127
This is a comprehensive directory providing information on over 8,000 major employers. The employers are listed by state. Data includes a description of each business, contact information, educational background requirements, common positions, and fringe benefits offered.

State Manufacturing Directories

Every state will have a directory. The directory can be found in most libraries or you may contact each state's Chamber of Commerce.

OTHER HELPFUL BOOKS

Who's Hiring Who, Author: Richard Lathrop
Published: Ten Speed Press, P.O. Box 7123, Berkely, CA 94707

What Color is Your parachute? Author: Richard Nelson Bolles
Published: Ten Speed Press, P.O. Box 7123, Berkeley, CA 94707

Rites of Passage at $100,000+, Author: John Lucht
Published: Viceroy Press, Inc., New York, NY

How To Teach Anyone Who Is Anyone, Author: Michael Levine
Published: Price/Stern Sloan
410 North La Cienega Blvd., Los Angeles, CA 90048

Jobs '97, Author: Kathryn & Ross Petras
Published: Simon & Schuster (Fireside)
Rockefeller Center, 1230 Avenue of the Americas, New York, NY 10020

National Survey of Professional, Administrative, Technical and Clerical Pay
Published annually by the Bureau of Labor Statistics (97 Pages)
Available: Government Printing Office, Bulletin 2208 S/N 029-001-02826-1, $4.75.
Summarizes an annual survey of selected professionals, technical, and clerical occupat-
ions in private industry. Includes occupational definitions used in the survey and a table
Which compares salaries in the private sector those in the federal government.

The American Almanac of Jobs and Salaries, Written: John W. Wright
Published: Avon Books (744 pages), $12.95
Includes job descriptions, salary ranges and advancement potential.

The Almanac of American Employers, Written: Jack W. Plunkett
Published: Contemporary Books, Chicago. (340 pages), $15.95
A guide to America's 500 most successful large corporations, profiled by rank in the area
of salaries, benefits, financial stability, and advancement opportunity.

How To Sell Yourself, Author: Joe Girard
Published: Warner Books, Inc., 75 Rockefeller Plaza, New York, NY 10010

NEWSPAPERS

It goes without saying that you will always want to consult the 'Help Wanted' ads in your
local newspaper. It might be possible for you to find an opportunity if your dreams in a
local paper. You must start reading the newspaper with a different slant than you have in
the past.

You could come across the opportunity of a lifetime on the front page, in the business section, editorial or sports section.

You may come across an article about new companies forming in your area. A large corporation setting up a branch office, a new store, a new restaurant, a new sports stadium, or a new product. With this information you should immediately begin to think about ways that you might become involved or contact these companies. Take advantage of the information you have read.

You can be assured that there is not a day that goes by her in America that a new product is not announced, or a new opportunity is presented by a company or individual. The more you read the more opportunities will make themselves available to you. Besides the local newspaper, you will want to start reading journals and publications in the area in which you are interested. There is probably a trade journal or publication in just about every industry in which you might be interested.

MAGAZINES

As with newspapers, you will find many stories about interesting and profitable companies in magazines. You will have to keep your career in mind when you are reading these publications. No matter what your interest there is probably a magazine on the newsstand that appeals to you. The only thing we can say here is to get these magazines and read them. You could find ideas and opportunities that could offer you insights into the 'Ideal Job' for you. Here are some magazines that may be helpful in your job search: Success, Fortune, Small Business Opportunities, Inc., Selling Power, Forbes, Time, Newsweek, Business Week, Money and Entrepreneur.

THE YELLOW PAGES

The Yellow Pages are another source of potential employers. You may look for 'Trade Associations' in your area of interest or specific field. The next step will be to contact the Trade Association for a membership directory. You may also want to review the category titles to find companies or products of interest and then contact employers that seem interesting.

STATE EMPLOYMENT SERVICES

Every state has a Department of Employment or Labor. These services are offered at no cost to you. You will find jobs or employment opportunities for all levels. In addition there are counseling, testing and placement services available. Consult the white pages of the telephone directory under state government listings in order to locate your local employment office.

Use the space below to list the agencies you are interested in contacting.

1. _____ .

2. _____ .

3. _____ .

ASSOCIATION INDEX

FEDERAL JOB INFORMATION CENTERS

The Federal Government employs over 1.5 million workers here in the United States and has employees in most foreign countries. The average income for this work force exceeds $30,000 a year. One important thing to keep in mind about government employment: Once you go to work for the government, it is next to impossible to be fired or laid off. In addition, it is not hard to advance up the ladder.

Additional information about government employment can be obtained from your nearest Library.. Look for the U.S. Government Manual. The book is lengthy but it offers information about every division of the government as well as lots of names of high level officials you can contact. You will need to take some time with this book.

To purchase the U.S. Government Manual, contact the U.S. Printing Office at 1-202-783-3238. You may want to visit the Federal Job Information Center of the U.S Ifuce if Personnel Management in your state. We are providing a listing of state offices, however, please check for current phone numbers as they change too fast to be accurate.

Institute of Financial Education
111 East Wacker Dr.
Chicago, Il 60601
312-644-3100

National Association of Bank Women
500 N. Michigan Ave., Suite 1400
Chicago, IL 60601
312-611-1700

American Society of Microbiology
1913 I Street N.W.
Washington, D.C. 20006

Academy of Television Arts and Sciences
3500 W. Olive Ave., Suite 700
Burbank, CA 91505
818-953-7575

American Sportscasters Association
150 Nassau St.
New York, NY 10038
212-227-8080

American Women in Radio and Television
1101 Connecticut Ave. N.W., Suite 700
Washington, D.C. 20036
202-429-5102

National Association of Broadcasters
1771 N. Street N.W.
Washington, D. C. 20036
202-429-5300

National Academy if Television Arts and Sciences
110 West Street
New York, NY 10019
212-586-8424

American Business Women's Association
91100 Ward Parkway
P.O. Box 8728
Kansas City, MO 64114
816-361-6621

American society of Professional and Executive Woman
1429 Walnut Street
Philadelphia, Pennsylvania 19102
215-563-4415

Industrial Chemical Research Association
1811 Monroe St.
Dearborn, MI 48124
313-464-4555

American Institute of Chemical Engineers
345 East 47th Street
New York, NY 10017
212-705-7496

American Chemical Society
1155 16th Street N.W.
Washington, D.C. 20036
202-872-4600

American Society of Civil Engineers
345 East 47th Street
New York, NY 10017
212-705-7496

National Association of Executive Secretaries
900 South Washington St., #g-13
Falls Church, VA 22046
703-237-8616

National Association for Legal Secretaries
2250 East 73rd Street, Suite 550
Tulsa, OK 74136
918-493-3540

National Association of Secretarial Services
100 Second Ave., South 604
St. Petersburg, FL. 33701
813-823-3646

Association of the Institute for Certification of Computer Professionals
2200 Devon Ave.
Des Plaines, IL 60018
312-299-4270

Association for Computing Machinery
11 West 42nd Street, 3rd Floor
New York, NY 10036
212-869-7440

National Cosmetology Association
3510 Olive Street
St. Louis, MO 63103
314-534-7980

National Shorthand Reporters Association
118 Park Street S.E.
Vienna, Virginia 22180
703-281-4677

International Credit Association
243 N. Lindbergh Blvd.
St. Louis, MO 63141
314-991-3030

National Association of Credit Management
520 8th Ave.
New York, NY 10018
212-947-5070

Data Processing Management Association
505 Busse Highway
Park Ridge, IL 60068
312-825-8124

American Dental Assistants Association
919 North Michigan Ave., Suite 3400
Chicago, IL 60611
312-664-3327

American Dental Hygienists
444 North Michigan Ave.
Chicago, IL 60611
312-440-8900

National Dental Technicians Association
P.O. Box 1236
Tulsa, OK 74101

American Dental Association
211 East Chicago Ave.
Chicago, IL 60611
312-440-2500

American Institute for Design and Drafting
966 Hungerford Dr., Suite 10B
Rockville, MD   20854
301-294-8712

National Association of Business Economists
28349 Chagrin Blvd.
Cleveland, OH   44122
216-464-7986

Institute of Electrical & Electronics Engineers
345 East 47th Street
New York, NY   10017
212-705-7900

Electronics Technicians Association International
604 N. Jackson
Greencastle, IN 46135
317-653-8262

Society of Women Engineers
United Engineering Center, Room 305
345 East 47th Street
New York, NY 10017
212-705-7855

International Association for Financial Planning
2 Concourse Parkway, Suite 800
Atlanta, GA 30329
404-395-1605

Women in Film
6464 Sunset Blvd.
Hollywood, CA 90028
213-463-6040

American Institute of Floral Designers
13 West Franklin Street
Baltimore, MD 21201
301-752-3318

International Chefs Association
P.O. Box 1889
New York, NY 10116
201-825-8455

National Restaurant Association
1200 17th Street N.W.
Washington, D.C. 20036
202-331-5900

Geological Society of America
P.O. Box 9140, Penrose Place
Boulder, CO 80301
303-447-2020

Graphic Arts Technical Foundation
4615 Forbes Ave.
Pittsburgh, PA 15213
412-621-6941

American Institute of Graphic Arts
1059 Third Ave.
New York, NY   10021
212-752-0813

American Home Economics Association
2010 Massachusetts Ave. N.W.
Washington, D.C.   20036
202-862-8300, 800-424-8080

American Hospital Association
840 N. Lake Shore Dr.
Chicago, IL   60611
312-280-6000

American Hotel and Motel Association
1201 New York Ave., Suite 600
Washington, D.C.   20005-3917
202-289-3100

American Society for Personnel Administration
606 North Washington St.
Alexandria, Virginia   22314
703-548-3440

Industrial Relations Research Association
7226 Social Science Building
University of Wisconsin
Madison, Wisconsin   53706
608-262-2762

American Academy of Actuaries
1720 I Street N.W.
Washington, D.C.   20006
202-223-8196

Independent Insurance Agents of American
100 Church Street, 19th Floor
New York, NY 10007
212-285-4250

American Society of Interior Designers
1430 Broadway
New York, NY 10018
212-944-9220

American Bar Association
750 North Lake Shore, Dr.
Chicago, IL 60611
312-988-5000

National Association of Legal Assistants
1601 South Main, Suite 300
Tulsa, OK 74120
917-587-6828

Environmental Management Association
1019 Highland Ave.
Largo, FL 33540
813-586-5710

American Telemarketing Association
5000 Van Nuys Blvd., Suite 200
Sherman Oaks, CA 91403
800-441-3335

American Marketing Association
250 South Wacker Dr., Suite 200
Chicago, IL 60606
312-648-0536

American Society of Mechanical Engineers
345 East 47th Street
New York, NY 10017
212-705-7722

American Association of Medical Assistants
20 North Wacker Drive, Suite 1575
Chicago, IL   60606
312-899-1500

American Medical Association
535 Dearborn Street
Chicago, IL   60606
312-645-5000

American Society of Metals, International
Metals Park, OH   44073
216-338-5151

National Association for Practical Nurse Education
1400 Spring Street, Suite 310
Silver Springs, MD   20916
301-588-2491

American Optometric Student Association
243 North Lindbergh
St. Louis, MO   63141
314-991-4100

American Society for Training and Development
P.O. Box 1443
1630 Duke Street
Alexandria, Virginia   22313
703-683-8100

American Petroleum Institute
1220 L. Street N.W.
Washington, D.C.   20005
202-682-8000

Student American Pharmaceutical Association
2215 Constitution Ave. N.W.
Washington, D.C.   20037
202-628-4410

Associated Photographers International
P.O. Box 4055
22231 Mulholland Highway, #19
Woodland Hills, CA   91365
818-888-9270

National Free Lance Photographers Association
10 South Pine Street
Doylestown, PA   18901
215-348-5578

American Psychological Association
1200 17th Street N.W.
Washington, D.C.   20036
202-955-7600

Public Relations Society of American
33 Irving Place
New York, NY 10003
212-995-2230

International Association of Business Communication
870 Market Street, Suite 940
San Francisco, CA   94102
415-433-3400

National Association of Purchasing Management
P.O. Box 2210
2055 East Centennial Circle
Tempe, AZ 85285-2160
602-752-NAPM

Institute of Real Estate Management
430 North Michigan Ave.
Chicago, IL 60611
312-661-1930

National Retail Merchants Association
100 West 31st Street
New York, NY 10001
212-244-8780

Sales and Marketing Executives International
Statler Tower, Suite 458
Cleveland, OH 44115
216-771-6650

National Association for Professional Saleswomen
P.O. Box 255708
Sacramento, CA 95865
916-484-1234

American Society for Industrial Security
1655 North Ft. Meyer Drive, Suite 1200
Arlington, VA 2209
703-522-5800

International Union of Tool, Die and Mold Makers
71 East Cherry Street
Rahway, N.J. 07065
201-388-3323

National Association of Business and Educational Radio
1501 Duke Street
Alexandria, Virginia 22134
703-739-0300

American Society of Travel Agents
1101 Ring Street
Alexandria, Virginia   2202
202-965-7520

International Association of Tour Managers
North American Region
1646 Chapel Street
New Haven, Connecticut   06511
203-777-5994

International Television Association
6311 North O'Connor Road, Suite 110
Irving, TX   75039
214-869-1112

American Society of Radiologic Technologists
15000 Central Avenue S.E.
Albuquerque, N.M.   87123
505-298-4500

American Society of Travel Agents
4400 Mac Arthur Blvd. N.W.
Washington, D.C.   20007
202-965-7520

American Welding Society
P.O. Box 351040
550 Lejeune Road N.W.
Miami, FL   33135
305-443-9353

OFFICE OF PERSONNEL MANAGEMENT
FEDERAL JOB INFORMATION CENTERS

ALABAMA: Huntsville
Southerland Building, 806 Governors Dr. S.W., 35801
Office Hours: M-F 9:00 a.m. to 4:00 p.m. (self-service)
205-544-5802, 24 hour recorded message

ALASKA: Anchorage
Federal Building, 701 C St. Room B118, 99513
Office Hours: Tuesday, Wednesday & Thursday, 11:00 a.m. to 1:00 p.m.
907-271-5821, 24 hour recorded message

ARIZONA: Phoenix
U.S. Postal Service Bldg, 522 W. Central Ave., 85004
Office Hours: M-F 9:00 a.m. to 12:00 p.m.
602-261-4736, 24 hour recorded message

ARKANSAS: Little Rock
Federal Building, 700 W. Capitol Ave., Room 3421, 72201
Office Hours: Monday, Tuesday, Thursday 12:00 p.m. to 4:00 p.m.
                           Wednesday & Friday, 8:00 a.m. to 4:00 p.m.
501-378-5842, 24 hour recorded message

CALIFORNIA: Los Angeles
Linder building, 845 S.Figueroa, 3rd Floor, 90017
Office Hours: M-F 9:00 a.m. 3:00 p.m. (closed 12:00-1:00 p.m.)
213-894-3360, 24 hour recorded message

Sacramento
1029 Q Street, Room 100, 95814
Office Hours: M-F 9:00 a.m. to 12:00 p.m.
916-551-1464, recorded message

San Diego
880 Front Street, Room 4-S-9, 92188
Office Hours: M - F 9:00 a.m. to 12:00 p.m.; (12:00 p.m. self serve)
619-293-6165, 24 hour recorded message

CALIFORNIA CONT.
San Francisco
211 Main St., Room 235, 94105
Office Hours: 9:00 a.m. to 12:00 p.m.
415-974-9725, 24 hour recorded message

COLORADO: Denver
P.O. Box 25167, 80225
12345 Alameda Pkwy, Lakewood, CO
Office Hours: M-F 9:00 a.m. to 3:45 p.m. (self service)
        Personal assistance 12:00 p.m. to 3:45 p.m.
303-236-4160 or 303-236-4161, 24 hour information
Request forms 24 hours a day, 303-236-4159
For the following states: North Dakota-303-236-4163; South Dakota
303-236-4164; Montana 303-236-4162; Utah 303-236-4165;
Wyoming 303-236-4166.
Request forms 24 hours a day, call 303-236-4159

CONNECTICUT: Hartford
Federal Building, 450 Main Street, Room 613, 06103
Office Hours: Monday-Thursday, 9:00 a.m. to 2:00 p.m.
203-722-3096; 24 hour recorded message @ 203-722-2320

DELAWARE: See Philadelphia, Pennsylvania listing.

DISTRICT OF COLUMBIA:
Metro Area:
1900 East Street, N.W. Room 1416, 20415
Office Hours: M-F 8:30 a.m. to 2:00 p.m.
202-653-8468, recorded message M-F 8:30 a.m. to 3:30 p.m.

FLORIDA: Orlando
Commodore Building, 3444 Mc Crory Place, Room 125, 32803-3712
Office Hours: M-f, 9:00 a.m. to 4:00 p.m. (self-service)
305-648-6148, 24 hour recorded message

GEORGIA: Atlanta
Richard B. Russell Federal Bldg

GEORGIA, CONT.:
    75 Spring Street S.W. Room 960, 30303
    Office Hours: M-F 9:00 a.m. to 4:00 p.m. (self service)
    404-331-4315, 24 hour recorded message

GUAM:
    Agana
    Pacific News Bldg, 238 O'Hara Street, Room 902, 96910
    Office Hours: M-F 9:30 a.m. to 12:00 p.m.
    472-7451, 24 hour recorded message

HAWAII:
    Honolulu (and other Hawaiian islands and overseas)
    Federal Bldg., 300 Ala Moana Blvd. Room 5316,   96850
    Office Hours: M-F 9:00 a.m. to 12:00 noon
    Oahu, 808-546-8600, 24 hour recorded message
    Other Hawaiian Islands and Overseas, 808-546-7108

IDAHO:
    See Washington listing

ILLINOIS:
    Chicago
    175 West Jackson Blvd., Room 519, 60604
    317-353-6192
    Office hours: M-F 8:00 a.m. to 4:30 p.m. (self service)
    M-F 9:00 a.m. to 12:00 noon
    312-353-6192, after telephone hours recorded message

INDIANA:
    Indianapolis
    Minton-Capehart Federal Bldg, 575 North Pennsylvania Ave., 46214
    Office Hours: M-F 7:00 a.m. to 6:00 p.m. (self service)
    Telephone service M-f 9:00 a.m. to 1:00 p.m., 317-269-7161
    312-353-7161, recorded message after telephone hours

IOWA:
    Des Moines
    210 Walnut Street, Room 191, 50309
    Office Hours: Monday, Wednesday, Friday 8:00 a.m. to 11:00 a.m.
    515-284-4545, recorded message
    Scott County, 312-353-5136
    Pottawattamie County, 402-221-3815

KANSAS: Whichita
One Twenty Bldg, 120 South Market Street, Room 101,   67202
Office Hours: M-F 9:00 a.m. to 12:00 noon;
Recorded Message: M-F, 9:00 a.m. to 3:00 p.m., 316-269-6106
In Johnson, Leavenworth, and Wyandotte Counties, 816-374-5702

KENTUCKY: See Ohio listing.

LOUISIANA: New Orleans
F. Edward Hebert Bldg, 610 South Maestri Place, Room 802, 701130
504-589-2764
Office Hours: M-F, 10:00 a.m. to 2:30 p.m. (closed 12:00—12:30)
Recorded message after hours: 504-589-2764

MAINE: See New Hampshire listing

MARYLAND: Baltimore
Garmatz Federal Bldg, 101 West Lombard Street,   21201
Office Hours: M-F 9:00 a.m. to 4:00 p.m.
Recorded message: 301-962-3822

D.C. area: See District of Columbia listing

MASSACHUSETTS: Boston
John W. McCormack Post Office and Courthouse (Lobby), 02109
Office Hours: M-F 9:00 a.m. to 4:00 p.m., 617-223-2571
617-223-1775 or 617-223-1776, 24 hour recorded message

MICHIGAN: Detroit
477 Michigan Ave., Room 565, 48226
Office Hours: M-F 8:00 a.m. to 4:00 p.m.
Telephone Service; M-F 12:00 noon to 4:00 p.m., 313-226-6950
Recording after telephone hours, 313-725-4430

MINNESOTA: Twin Cities
Federal Bldg, Ft. Snelling, Twin Cities, 55111
Office Hours: M-F, 9:00 a.m. to 12:00 noon
Telephone Service; M-F 12:30 p.m. to 3:30 p.m., 612-725-4430

MISSISSIPPI: Jackson
100 West Capitol Street, Suite 335, 39269
Office Hours: M-F 9:00 a.m. to 1:00 p.m., telephone 601-965-4585
Recording after office hours: 601-965-4585

MISSOURI: Kansas City
Federal Bldg., 601 East 12th Street, Room 134, 64106
Office Hours: Monday, Wednesday Friday, 8:00 a.m. to 11:00 a.m.
Recorded message: 816-374-5702

St. Louis
Old Post Office, 815 Olive Street, Room 400, 63101
Office Hours: Monday, Wednesday, Friday, 8:00 a.m. to 11:00 a.m.
Recorded message: 314-425-4380

MONTANA: See Colorado Listing

NEBRASKA: Omaha
U.S. Courthouse and Post Office Building, 215 North 17th Street
Room 1010, 68102
Office hours: Monday, Wednesday, Friday, 9:00 a.m. to 12:00 noon
Recorded message: M-F, 9:oo a.m. to 3:00 p.m., 402-221-3815

NEVADA: See Sacramento, California listing

NEW HAMPSHIRE: Portsmouth
Thomas J. McIntyre Federal Bldg., 80 Daniel Street, Room 104 03801
603-433-0763
Office Hours: Monday—Thursday, 9:00 a.m. to 2:00 p.m.
402-221-3815, 24 hour recorded message

NEW JERSEY: Newark
Peter W. Rodino, Jr. Federal Bldg, 970 Broad Street, Room 104, 07102
Office Hours: M-F 9:30 a.m. to 4:30 p.m.
Recorded message M-F , 8:30 a.m. to 5:00 p.m., 201-645-3673
In Camden, 215-597-7440

NEW MEXICO: Albuquerque
Federal Bldg, 421 Gold Ave., South West, 87102
Office Hours: Monday—Thursday, 8:00 a.m. to 12:00 noon
505-766-5583, 24 hour recorded message
In Dona Ana, Otero, and El Paso Counties: 505-766-1893

NEW YORK: New York City
Jacob K Javits Federal Building, 26 Federal Plaza, 10278
Office hours: M-F, 8:30 a.m. to 4:00 p.m.
Recorded message: M-F, 7:30 a.m. to 4:00 p.m., 212-264-0422

Syracuse:
James N. Hanley Federal Bldg, 100 South Clinton Street, 13260
Office Hours: M-F, 9:00 a.m. to 3:00 p.m., 315-423-5660

NORTH CAROLINA: Raleigh
Federal Bldg., 310 Bern Ave., P.O. Box 25069, 27611
Office hours: M-F, 9:00 a.m. to 4:00 p.m. (self service)
919-856-4361, 24 hour recorded message

NORTH DAKOTA: See Colorado listing.

OHIO: Dayton
Federal Bldg., 200 West 2nd Street, 45402
Office hours: Monday, Tuesday, Thursday, Friday, 10:00 a.m. to 2:00 p.m.
Telephone service: M-F, 8:00 a.m. to 11:00 a.m., 513-225-2720
Recording after telephone hours: 513-225-2720

OKLAHOMA: Oklahoma City
200 N.W. Fifth Street, Room 205, 73102
Office hours: Monday—Thursday, 10:00 a.m. to 3:00 p.m.,
(closed 12:00 noon to 1:00 p.m.)
405-231-4948, 24 hour recorded message

OREGON: Portland
Federal Building, 1220 South West Third Street, Room 376, 97204
Office hours: M-f, 12:00 noon to 3:00 p.m.
503-221-3141, 24 hour recorded message

PENNSYLVANIA: Harrisburg

Federal Bldg., Room 168, P.O. Box 761, 17108
Office hours: Monday, Tuesday, Thursday, Friday, 8:00 a.m. to 12:00 noon
717-782-4494

Philadelphia
Wm J. Green, Jr. Federal Bldg. 600 Arch Street, Room 1416, 19106
Office hours: M-F, 9:00 a.m. to 3:30, p.m., 215-597-7440

Pittsburgh
Federal Bldg., 1000 Liberty Ave., Room 119, 15222
Office hours; M-F, 9:00 a.m. to 4:00 p.m.
Recorded message, 412-644-2755

PUERTO RICO: San Juan

Federico Depetau Federal Bldg., Carlos E. Chardon Street,
Hato Rey, P.R. 00918
Office hours: Monday, Wednesday, Friday, 8:30 a.m. to 12:00 noon
Recorded message, M-F, 7:30 a.m. to 4:00 p.m., 809-753-4209

RHODE ISLAND: Providence

John D. Pastore Federal Bldg., Room 310, Kennedy Plaza, 02903
Office hours: Monday—Wednesday, 10:00 a.m. to 1:00 p.m.
401-428-5251

SOUTH CAROLINA: Charleston

334 Meeting Street, 29403
Office hours: M-F, 9:00 a.m. to 4:00 p.m. (self service)
803-724-4328, 24 hour recorded message

SOUTH DAKOTA : See Colorado listing

TENNESSEE: Memphis

100 North Bldg., Suite 1312, 38103
Office hours: M-F, 9:00 a.m. to 4:00 p.m. (self service)
901-521-3956, 24 hour recorded message

TEXAS: Dallas
1100 Commerce Street, Room 6B4, 75242
Office hours: M-F, 10:00 a.m. to 3:00 p.m. (closed 12:00 noon to 1:00 p.m.)
214-767-8035, 24 hour recorded message

Houston
701 San Jacinto Street, 4th Floor, 77002
Office hours: Monday , Tuesday, Thursday, Friday, 8:00 a.m. to 12:00 p.m.
713-226-2375, 24 hour recorded message

San Antonio
643 East Durango Blvd., 78206
Office hours: M-F, 8:00 a.m. to 12:00 noon
512-229-6611 or 512-229-6600, 24 hour recorded message

UTAH: See Colorado listing.

VERMONT: See New Hampshire listing.

VIRGINIA: Norfolk
Federal Bldg., 200 Granby Mall, Room 220, 23510
Office hours: M-F, 9:00 a.m. to 4:00 p.m. (self service)
804-441-3355, 24 hour recorded message

D. C. area See the District of Columbia listing

WASHINGTON: Seattle
Federal bldg., 915 Second Ave., 98174
Office hours: M-F, 9:00 a.m. to 12:00 noon (self service)
   12:00 noon to 3:30 p.m.
206-442-4365, 24 hour recorded message

WEST VIRGINIA: Charleston
Federal Bldg., 500 Quarrier Street, Room 1017, 25301
Office hours: Tuesday-Friday, 12:00 noon to 4:00 p.m.
Recorded message 304-347-5174

WISCONSIN: Counties of Grant, Iowa, Lafayette, Dane, Green, Rock, Jefferson, Wal worth, Waukesha, Racine, Kenosha, and Milwaukee, call 312-353-6189 All other Wisconsin residents refer to the Minnesota listing.

WYOMING: See Colorado Listing

FUNCTIONS OF THE JOB INFORMATION CENTERS

Here is how the Job Information Centers work. The Federal Job Opportunity List publishes a list on the 1st and 15th of each month. The Federal Job List has job openings in local areas as well as selected positions nationwide and worldwide.

You will find that these lists are very lengthy so they will only be posted. A copy will not be available. Review each listing and make notes on the jobs that are of interest to you. Each job description will tell you how to apply, the grade level, pay, location, number of vacancies, and how to get the forms to apply for the position.

The starting grade level is GS-1 which as a pay level is about the same as minimum wage. A GS-12 grade level pays approximately $16.00 an hour. It is possible, with experience and time on the job, to be promoted to a GS-18 grade level which pays approximately $68,000 per year or higher.

After you have checked the list and found something interest, you can also contact the State Employment Service. They have a copy of the Federal Job Opportunity list. Obtain the nearest State Employment Service location to obtain a copy.

No one agency of the government does the hiring. You will have to apply to each division that has a job of interest to you. The application process is similar to a private sector job. You have to interview and sell yourself. 'Networking' can help you get your foot in the door. Like the private sector, many times knowing someone will help you get the job.

You may want to consider visiting the offices of your U.E. Representative and/or your U.S. Senator. Inform your representative or Senator that you would appreciate any help that they may be able to give, for example an introduction to anyone they might know in the agency that you are interested in working for. You may be surprised with the help you may get. Be sure that you have the name of the agency, location, and name of the hiring authority before you ask for such a favor.

It is necessary when you apply for a Federal job that you submit form SF171 which is essentially a government application form. The forms are available where you find the Federal Job Opportunity List. The form m must be completed before you go to an interview. You will also want to take your resume which reflects your skills and experiences toward the job description you are responding to. Like responding to a private sector job, you will want to show how your job experience and qualifications make you the best suited for the position.

For every position you find of interest from the Federal Job Opportunity List, you will want to fill out a separate copy of the 'Prospective Employer Information and Follow-up Form.'

NOTE: For additional information about Federal Jobs, read the Directory of Employment Opportunities in the Federal Government by Stephen E. Vogel. It is published by Arco Publishing, Inc., 215 Park Ave. South, New York, NY 10003.

WARNING   WARNING   WARNING

You may find ads in the newspapers throughout the country which may read something like the following:

"Government Jobs" $15,400 to $72,500, now hiring!

These ads are not placed by Government agencies. They are placed by people selling information. They have no authority to hire, and you can get all the information you need about Government jobs from the agencies' addresses provided in earlier pages.

IDENTIFYING THE SPECIFIC JOB OR THE IDEAL JOB

We have asked you to do some research and to find out information about a company or organization you have heard about or read about in the newspaper. We are now going to give you some ideas as to how to proceed after researching the job and company.

1. First, contact someone you might know in the company or organization. Get on the phone and talk with everyone you know. 'Networking,' right? Then get the name of an employee. Let us say this: we can see you saying to yourself, "What are these nuts talking about; this is a lot of work," Right! Think for a minute how many others out there are going to do this. Not many. No one said this was going to be easy. Not us! The only one who is going to benefit from this is YOU!

2. After you have gotten the name, call the person and introduce yourself. Tell him/her who suggested you call them. Then ask if he/she knows the name of the person who is the decision-maker on hiring. It would be to your advantage to discuss the job description. If this person does not know, get another contact within the organization and continue to do your networking until you get the answers to all your questions. It would be beneficial if you record every name and all comments.

3. Next you will want to visit the organization if at all possible. We are aware of the fact there may be limitations as to logistics, time, and money. But if at all possible, you want to know if you will fit in. Are the people you meet the kind of people you would like to work with? Are they friendly, receptive, and smiling? Do the employees look happy to be employed there? Is the overall environment inviting.

While you are there, you can confirm what you know or get answers to questions you do not know, discuss the job description, get financial reports, product brochures, and the company's business. If possible, find out if the position is a new one or if it is replacing a terminated employee. Find out the name of the person if you can so that you might contact him/her.

You might ask, "Well, who should I talk to?" Talk to everyone from the 'gate-keeper' (secretary) to the janitor. Ask them if they are happy with their job. Be a good 'listener.' This can be invaluable in getting people to respond to you.

Listening makes people feel important. People also enjoy helping others when given the opportunity. The receptionist can be very good sources of information. They are out in front exposed to a lot that is going on in the organization. They normally have the position because they are very outgoing and willing to talk.

If you still come up short with regard to information about the company, ask the receptionist for the name of the nicest person in the Personnel Department. Next, go to the department and ask for this person. Tell this person you were told that he/she was identified as the nicest person in the department. You have given the individual a reputation to live to; hopefully they will. Inform him/her that you are applying for the _____ position. Ask if there is a written job description, or if someone could explain what the organization is looking for. You can also ask about the person that had the position. Was this person promoted, downsized, or did they quit? What you learn about the ex-employee, such as punctuality and absenteeism, you can incorporate these issues in your cover letter. If you do contact the employee, you can compare their story with those that you heard. You may decide after your research that you may not find this job to your liking. On the other Hand, you may indeed discover that this could be your 'ideal job.'

Now that you have decided that this is an organization you would like to work for, make sure you a copy of the 'Job Application for Employment.' You will also want to discover What degree of testing will be involved in applying for said position. This could also be a good time to ask for the salary range.

4. You can go to the library and check out the company, its financial strength, ownership, officers, product, time in business, branches, and other valuable information. Consult Dunn & Bradstreet Directories, Fitch Corporation, Moody's Industrial Manual, Standard and Poor's Register of Corporations, Thomas' Register of American Manufacturers, and Who's Who in Finance and Industry. You may find the name of the contact in your search listed in one of the Who's Who books.

Any time you have trouble finding information at the library, see the reference librarian. He/she works with this information everyday and will be able to direct you very quickly to the sources you need to check out.

5. If you are to work for a national company at a new branch, take the time to visit and talk to the employees as we indicated above. Of course, it is necessary to

locate phone numbers and addresses of branches in other cities or states. You can call and talk to people who hold the position you are applying for in other areas to gain their help and information. Before you call, make sure that you have all the questions written down to save their time, and of course your time, your trou ble and phone costs.

6. You can visit competitors of the firm you intend to interview. Tell them your intent; be honest. Ask them their opinion. We would say that in most cases they will be truthful although some of the information may not be totally objective. You will find out things you did not know.

7. A lot of work, right? It sure is, but we do not want tot do this again if we can help it. Go home, take the information you have and put together a 'knock them dead' cover letter and resume. You will have some valuable experience to take forward. You will get better and better the more times you do this.

You will have discovered a networking system, and the employer may delay running an ad or contacting an employment agency in lieu of discussing future openings with you as a result of your phone call.

CHAPTER NINE

Self Employment

Self-employment is always an avenue that a person who is looking for work may want to consider. The best idea is to be very careful about what business you are looking into. It always pays to look before you leap. You should do research before you put down any of your hard-earned cash. Many people have been burned by going into business for themselves without doing product and market evaluation. Be sure you are doing the right thing. Service businesses are the easiest to get going with limited finances.

The types of business out there are unlimited, however, considering some type of service business may be the best since there is little outlay for inventory. Inventory can be expensive and can kill your business. The scope of this book is not to examine going into business, however, we will touch on a few details that may be helpful to you.

You may want to consider a franchise operation especially if the franchise agrees to train you and get you started in business for a fixed fee. Ninety percent of all new small businesses will fail in the first five years. The reason given for this is usually money (or the lack of it). The reason is seldom lack of money, but rather lack of management training or experience. The manager must be trained in how to get funding. There is a great deal of money or venture capital out there if you are familiar with the business and have a great, well-developed and thought-out business plan. Some businesses that fail do so because they look good to the 'new' entrepreneur, but either he/she has not done their 'homework' as to the feasibility of the business or he/she is totally lacking in management skills. Ninety percent of all franchises will survive the first five years. The reason for this is that they have researched the target market, provide training, provide great products and outstanding management.

You must stay in business for at least five years as a 'rule of thumb' before you can make any real money. This is called the 'break even point.' You must hang in there or you will wipe out early in the game! You can expect to start making money after five years of hard work in almost any business. There are many franchises; therefore, you will want to investigate each one completely to determine which one is the right 'fit' for you. You will need to ask a lot of questions and get written answers to all of them to your satisfaction.

The hardest part of going into business is finding quali-fied customers who can buy or use your products and services. People must have enough money to keep their business afloat long enough to get proper market exposure. It has been estimated that to get a business going, you have to be able to stay in business more than three years without making any profit. Other sources say it takes three to five years to get a business going. We are not going to tell you how long it will take to get your business launched, but only to suggest that you are careful in this undertaking. There are too many variables to consider and each one of you have different needs and talents. Having your own business does have many rewards which you many want consider. The most obvious reward is money down the road. Another reward may be time off.

If you have decided to start your own business, it is important to develop a plan. The scope of this book is not to teach how to develop a business plan which is a whole book of itself. However, a business plan leads to a sound business structure. The Plan provides the opportunity to consider alternatives and select the best one for the type of business and owner's needs. Most businesses fail because the entrepreneur did not plan carefully before starting his/her business. It is tragic to realize that many-if not most– entrepreneurs charge headlong into opening the doors of their new businesses thinking they will be able to learn as to go along. This is clearly not so.

With the 'Business Plan,' the business owner is in a better position to balance his/her personal needs against the advantages and limitations of each type of organization. It is for this reason that we suggest that you take additional steps necessary in the development of a small business that will help you in the quest for personal success. The business plan along with a 'Marketing Plan' are important steps you should take to realize your goals.

Many millionaires were people like you; most did not win the lotto or inherit the money. Most millionaires today went into business for themselves. It is very difficult to make a lot of money working for someone else. The reason is obvious, the owner always gets the profit not the workers who make it happen. You may make a comfortable living but usually you will not become rich. If you like to call the shots and take risks you may want to have your own business. Remember that the average millionaire has gone broke eight times before hitting the big time. Hard work pays off in the long haul. You must keep trying!

You must be ready to change your plans quickly as opportunities avail themselves. Opportunities come and go all the time. Remember you are looking for the 'best' deal for your future. No one rings a bell to announce that a job is available.

No one will ever look out for your interest better than you, your family and friends. Your place of employment will look for its best interest which may not necessarily be your best interest. You have to look out for you! You can only trust one person every day to look out for you, and that person is YOU!

SELF ASSESSMENT

During your self-assessment, consider the following 'personality profile' of the successful entrepreneur:

- Tough mindedness-the entrepreneur must be able to make and stick to decisions.

- Willingness to work-You must work harder and longer than anyone else in the business

- Self-confidence-You must feel no threat to your authority.

- Willing to take 'reasonable' risks-the entrepreneur must be able to take risks based upon intelligent limits.

- Flexibility-As an entrepreneur, you have to be able to juggle many hats.

- Creativity-You have to be able to see problems as opportunities.

- Goal setting-The successful entrepreneur strives to make things come true.

- Problem solving-You have the ability to chart a path to success.

- Desire for profit-remember, profit is not a bad word. Be efficient with your resources.

- Enthusiasm-Avoid negativism.

CHAPTER TEN

Temporary Employment

Sometimes the only way you can go to work for the 'ideal' company is by going to work for a temporary help agency and being placed in a temporary vacancy. Fact is, some companies have this type of hiring policy. And the way it looks, this is going to be the trend for a long while since it is working for many large corporations.

Here is why it looks good to many companies. First, the firm does not have to pay for benefits or employee taxes. If the employee does not meet the expectations, he/she can be immediately replaced. Companies do not have to take 'risks' when they are hiring; they are getting a known commodity. The companies can try any number of individuals on a given job until they find one that fits their needs. They can offer that person a full-time position.

This is ideal from the employer's standpoint. Are there any advantages for you? Sure, but you have to maintain an outstanding attitude and understand that you have to do your best on each assignment as these will be the only people who will be offered positions with full benefits. The temporary position may provide you with additional experience, it gives you immediate income, and a major advantage, it allows you to take a look at the workings and the operations of the 'ideal' company without making a major commitment. It may or may not be what you are really looking for and now you have a painless way to find out.

Remember, temporary agencies will test your skills at no charge, so it is also a means of checking the proficiency of some of your skills. This can be especially helpful if you have been absent from the job market for a while.

The temporary agencies earn their pay by performing a screening service for the employers and providing them with qualified candidates for specific jobs. You must sell yourself to the agency much as you would if you were interviewing directly to the employer. Before you contact a temporary agency, make sure you are familiar with all phases of job search.

Record Names of Temporary Agencies Below

Agency:_____Phone:_____
Address:_____

Agency:_____Phone:_____
Address:_____

Agency:_____Phone:_____
Address:_____

Agency:_____Phone:_____
Address:_____

CHAPTER ELEVEN

The Small Business: It Could Be Your

"Ideal Job'

Your 'dream' may be to work for a Fortune 500 company. The real fact is, throughout the 1980's and into the 1990's, this country's giants like Xerox, IBM, Boeing and numerous others have been or are continuing to lay off hundreds and even thousands of employees. The total number of persons who have lost their job can be in the millions a year.

The fact that small and medium-sized companies are now emerging as the key creative force in our nation's economy. Smaller-scale firms with less than 250 employees have climbed to employ early seventy percent of the total work force of the United States. It has been estimated that this trend will continue into the millennium.

If you are like most American, you may have a desire to have your own business some-day. If so, paying your dues with t he smaller company could be exactly the apprentice-ship you are looking for. When you work for a small, you often have the opportunity to learn every aspect of a business operation. When you work for a giant firm, you may get pigeon-holed and not have the same opportunities.

The entrepreneur is today's folk hero of modern business life. Not only do they provide jobs, introduce innovations, and spark economic growth they offer many opportunities for employment and training. The entrepreneur is no longer viewed as a dull purveyor of gro-ceries or auto parts. Instead they are seen as energizers who take risks necessary in grow-ing a productive economy. Each year, thousands of such individuals from teenagers to senior citizens launch new businesses of their own providing the dynamic leadership that leads to economic progress.

The entrepreneur may not only e the founder of the business but for definition it also includes all active owner-managers. This also includes second generation members of family owned firms and owner-manager who buy out the founders of existing firms. So not only can you learn and earn from working for a small firm, but you might be able to purchase said company if the conditions are correct without starting from scratch to generate a new business yourself.

No matter how or why you got to the small business you will get a chance to examine the kinds of opportunities that exist. You will also have an opportunity to explore how attractive the rewards of being an entrepreneur might be. This is true at least for the company or business you are associated with.

You must remember, entrepreneurs possess special characteristics in order to succeed, you are going to have to do a lot of self-assessment to determine if you have these characteristics. Another important point which is often overlooked is to determine if it is the 'right time' to launch a new business. This point was brought home when one of the authors launched a business in the oil industry shortly after the major crash in 1980, only to discover that it was impossible to give equipment away let alone sell it. It goes without saying a 'great idea' became a disaster and the business was closed after a few short months.

What kind of entrepreneurs (small business owners) are there and what types of businesses do they operate? We will explore these questions and see if we can put these questions into perspective. We will look at a few individuals that have had successful ventures, this approach may give you a feel for the possibility that can be achieved in your own dream of having your own business. These examples demonstrate the continued existence of opportunities and show the vast potential for new ventures. Remember, all business ventures may not be spectacular but can still provide highly attractive career options!

The medical industry is a billion dollar business. Many companies and organizations are multi-million operations, such as hospitals, insurance companies, HMO's etc. However, within this industry there are many entrepreneurial organizations and businesses. In Irvine California, a pharmacist established OSO Home Care Inc, in 1983. OSO Home Care is independently owned and provides the highest quality of pharmaceutical products and services throughout Southern California. OSO was formed to meet the growing need for home intravenous therapy, medical surgical supplies, and medical equipment as an economic alternative to prolonged hospital care. OSO Home Care prides itself in their ability to stay on the leading edge if all the latest pharmaceutical developments.

Currently, OSO offers a full range of intravenous and nutritional therapies for home use. OSO has grown from a Mom and Pop operation in 1983 to a five million dollar operation today. Both the pharmacist and his wife play an active role in the business to insure its continued growth. Throughout the United States, home services for pharmaceuticals and medical supplies exists. In the medical industry there are opportunities in hospice care, medical equipment sales, private duty nursing, nutrition therapy, physical therapy, occupational and speech therapy. Be aware that many areas of health care are subject to strict licensing requirements and possibly review and certification by government and state agencies.

From a start-up business in 1973, Federal Express Corporation has grown to be a $7 billion dollar company. It is a relatively new business as far as businesses are concerned. Federal Express originated in the mind of Frederic W. Smith, a student at Yale. In 1965, he wrote a paper for an economics course proposing a new type of air freight service. According to his thesis, which later proved successful a company with its own planes dedicated to freight distribution should be superior to existing freight forwarders who were limited by the shifting schedules of passenger airlines.

by
fi-

This venture has been unique in many ways. The business was forced to start with a fleet of planes that could cover the entire country. The founder also came from a wealthy family and was able, as well as willing to risk a substantial part of the family fortune investing several million dollars. Nevertheless, the nancing requirements were great and Smith found it necessary to obtain the major portion of the financing from the venture capital industry. As the business developed over a dozen equity groups participated in three major rounds of financing.

Although the start-up was unusual in many ways, it is especially significant in showing the ability of one person, a potential entrepreneur, to conceptualize an entirely new type of business studying business methods and new trends. Smith's concept was implemented so successfully that it changed the very way in which business in America communicates and ships its freight. Over the years we have seen a number of companies large and small move into the delivering of freight. Today there are several well known names in this industry.

After spending some time at a small Alabama college, Barbara Gardner Proctor found a job as an advertising copywriter in Chicago. As she gained experience in advertising, she also developed an appreciation for quality in advertising.

One particular concept suggested for a TV commercial struck her as tasteless and offensive this difference of opinion lead to her being fired. Following her dismissal she was able to get a loan fro the Small Business Administration for $80,000 and she was on her way to opening her own business. She opened her agency in 1970. Today, still relatively small, she is well respected in her industry. She specializes in advertising, public relations, and event management. Serving accounts like Kraft Foods, Sears, and Chicago's big Jewel Food Stores she has found her niche in which she can compete effectively and be true to her own values.

We have known a number of individuals with an entrepreneurial spirit some in the industrial arena, food industry, manufacturing and several other areas. Their personalities are all different but they all have one thing in common-they all were willing to take risks and prefer to be their own boss.

In a private enterprise system as we have here in America, any individual is free to enter business for himself or herself. At any time there could be potentially profitable opportunities existing in our environment. It is important that these opportunities be recognized and acted upon.

Rewards and Drawbacks

There are a number of reasons why individuals are 'pulled' toward becoming an entrepreneur. These rewards may be grouped, for the sake of simplicity, into three basic categories: profit; independence; and a satisfying life-style.

Profit

The financial status of any business must compensate its owner for investing his/her time and personal savings in the business before any 'true profits' are realized. The person who goes into business expects a return that will not only compensate them for the time and money they invest, but also reward them <u>well</u> for their risk and initiative taken in operating their own business. The profit incentive is the most powerful motivator for most entrepreneurs. The truth in many cases, the dream of wealth and profit may never materialize. More than sixty-five percent (65%) of the companies that go into business are in bankruptcy after five (5) years.

Independence

It is true there are many of us out there that welcome the freedom to operate independently. For many this is an important motivating factor. In a survey of small-business owners, thirty-eight percent (38%) of those that left their jobs left because they wanted to be their own boss. Many of these entrepreneurs have a strong desire to make their own decisions, take risks, and reap the rewards. Being one's own boss seems an attractive ideal. The author recalls working for a compressed air and pump firm in the 1980's where more than twenty-five percent (25%) of the sales staff spun off to start their own business.

Of course, independence does not guarantee an easy life. Most entrepreneurs work very hard for long hours and in many instances receive no pay in the beginning. However, they do have the satisfaction of making their own decisions within the constraints imposed by economic and other environmental factors. In talking to many independent businessmen across the country we frequently hear about the personal satisfaction they feel in regard to owning their own business. Some even refer to their business as "fun." As an entrepreneur myself, this author can identify with the "fun" attitude. There is an enjoyment derived from the independence as well as making the 'deal' or closing that sale, and writing yourself that paycheck.

Drawbacks of Entrepreneurship

Although there are many rewards, there are also drawbacks and costs associated with business ownership. Starting and operating one's business typically demands hard work, long hours, and much emotional energy. Business ownership is described as exciting but very demanding. There are major strains on the family which need to be taken into consideration. There is always the possibility of the business failing. This is a constant strain on the entrepreneur and the family. As we have indicated, the entrepreneur must assume a variety of risks, no one likes to be a loser. I recall how I felt when I had to close my corporation back in the 1980's.

Characteristics of Entrepreneurs

The common stereotype of the entrepreneur emphasizes such characteristics as a high need for achievement, a willingness to take moderate risks, and a strong sense of self-confidence. As we look at specific entrepreneurs, we see individuals who for the most part, fit this image. This author has known many entrepreneurs over the years and have found that most could be described as loners, had a difficult time working for others, and wanted the freedom to come and go as they please. In addition, most were money motivated and did not like to take orders. However, we must express two words of caution, first, scientific proof of the importance of these characteristic sis lacking, and second, there are exceptions to every rule. Individuals who do not 'fit the mold' may still be successful as entrepreneurs.

Need for Achievement

Psychologists recognized that people differ in the degree of their need for achievement. Individuals with low need for achievement are those who seem to be contented with their present status. On the other hand, individuals with a high need for achievement like to compete with some standard of excellence and prefer to be personally responsible for their own assigned tasks. In a leading study on achievement motivation, there did appear to be a positive correlation between the need for achievement and entrepreneurial activity. It has been suggested that those who become entrepreneurs have, on the average, a higher need for achievement.

Willingness to take Risks

There is a risk that all entrepreneurs must take when starting and/or operating their business. These risks will vary from business to business. The stress and the time required in starting and running a business will place the family at risk. You may be willing to make the sacrifice, but your family may not. This author can recall many evenings during which I enlisted the help of my children to lick hundreds of envelopes and packaging products for mailing. There is a point that these activities are unwelcome tasks especially in the beginning when there may be little to no reward. You may be building your future business, while at the same time destroying your family. In some situations the outcome depends on pure luck.

Self-confidence

Individuals who possess self-confidence feel they can meet the challenges that confront them. They have a sense of mastery over the types of problems they might encounter. Studies indicate that successful entrepreneurs tend to be self-confident individuals who see the potential problems in launching a new venture but believe in their own ability to overcome these problems.

Entrepreneurial Opportunity

There is no substitute for education and experience as part of the necessary preparation for most entrepreneurs. Although requirements vary with the nature and demands of a particular business, but there is a requirement for some 'know how.' Besides having experience, additionally prospective entrepreneurs must build their financial resources in order to make the initial investment. This author can recall when I was in your shoes, many friends and acquaintances telling me "why don't you go into business for yourself?" This sounded simple to my friend advisers however, without financial resources, research, experience and motivation I could not easily 'run off' and start a business.

Although there are no hard and fast rules concerning the right age for starting a business, some age deterrents exist. Young people may be discouraged from entering entrepreneurial careers by inadequacies in preparation and resources. On the other hand, older people develop family, financial and job commitments that make entrepreneurship seem too risky. As much 'fun' as it was to have my own corporation this author would have to think long and hard about building a new business. For other older people, there is a stronger interest in acquiring retirement benefits and/or higher positions within their organization with rewards of greater responsibilities and higher salaries.

The ideal time for starting a business appears to lie somewhere between the late 20's and early 40's when there is a balance between preparatory experiences on the one hand and family obligations on the other. But I understand why Colonel Sanders did not really get going until he was 72 years old. Obviously, there are exceptions to this generalization. Some teenagers start their own firms (consider the web sites popping up on the internet). For other persons at ages 50 or 60 they walk away from successful careers in big business when they become excited by the prospects of entrepreneurship.

Anticipating the Event

Many potential entrepreneurs never take the fateful step of launching their own business ventures. Some, like this author, actually make the move stimulated by precipitating events such as a job termination, job dissatisfaction, or an unexpected opportunity.

Loss of a job for example, caused the author to start my own business in North Salt Lake, Utah. I had been a General Manager for a machine repair company. I was well educated, having achieved a Masters Degree, I had years of experience in sales and marketing. I found myself in the early 1980's looking for a job. After several months of job hunting I decided to strike out on my own and develop a business in the oil industry.

Losing a job is only one of many types of experiences that may serve as a catalyst to 'taking the plunge' as an entrepreneur. Some individuals become so disenchanted with formal academic programs that they simply walk away from the classroom and start new lives as entrepreneurs. Others become exasperated with the rebuffs of perceived injustices at the hands of superiors in large organizations and leave in disgust to start their own businesses.

In a more positive vein, prospective entrepreneurs may unexpectedly stumble across business opportunities. A friend may offer, for example, to sponsor an individual as an Amway distributor. Or a relative may suggest that the individual leave a salaried position and take over a family business. Many prospective entrepreneurs, of course, simply plan for and seek out independent business opportunities. There is little in the way of precipitating events involved in their decision to become entrepreneurs. We cannot say what proportion of new entrepreneurs make their move because of some particular event. However, many who launch new firms or otherwise go into business for themselves are obviously helped along by precipitous events.

Preparing for the Career as an Entrepreneur

It is important that we mix the right amount of education and experience. How much or what kind of each is necessary is notoriously difficult to specify. Dave Thomas, President of Wendy's Hamburgers, started when he was 15 working in restaurants. After meeting and helping to establish Kentucky Fried Chicken with the Colonel, he 'spun off' and developed his Wendy's empire.

Different types of ventures call for different types of preparation. The background or skills needed to start a company to produce computer software are obviously different from those needed to open an automobile garage. There are also striking differences in the backgrounds of those who succeed in the same industry. For these reasons, we must be cautious in discussing qualifications, realizing there are exceptions to every rule.

Some fascinating entrepreneurial success stories feature individuals who dropped out of school to start their ventures. This should not lead one to conclude, however, that education is generally unimportant. Research tells us that new business owners formal education is superior to that of the general adult public. In recent years, we have seen colleges and universities greatly expanding their offerings in entrepreneurship and small business. Now thousands of students across the country are taking how-to-start-your-own-business courses.

Business owners themselves identify three general factors that business owners regarded as important.

    1; **Entrepreneurial value** - intuition, extroversion, risk taking, creativity, flexibility, a sense of independence, and a high value of time.

    2. **Managerial skills** - niche strategy, effective management of cash flow, a simple but efficient budgetary system, pre-ownership experience, education, and a simple organization structure.

    3. **Interpersonal skills** - good relationship with a credit officer or banker, good customer service relations, and good employee relations.

Types of Entrepreneurships

The field of small business takes in a large variety of entrepreneurs and entrepreneurial ventures. We are going to review a number of entrepreneurships by identifying various types of people and the firms that are out there.

New Wave if Entrepreneurs

The new wave of entrepreneurs are women. Their presence has risen dramatically over the last two decades. We have seen a growth of 57.4 percent increase of women-owned businesses the business receipts rising by 81.2 percent. In the United States women own 28 percent of the businesses and employ 10 percent of the nation's workers. Woman are opening beauty shops, clothing stores, and the women ownership of construction firms rose by nearly 60 percent and their ownership of manufacturing firms more than doubled between 1982 and 1987.

Women do face barriers, some women find limited opportunities finding business relationships with others in similar positions. It takes time and effort for them to gain full acceptance and to develop informal relationships with others in local, mostly male, business and professional groups. Women are attacking this problem by increasing their participation in predominantly male organizations and also by forming networks of their own –the female equivalent of the 'old network.'

Franchises

Because of the constraints and guidance provided by contractual relationships with franchising organizations, the franchise functions as a limited entrepreneur.

Franchising has many advantages and disadvantages to them. It is not the within the scope of this book to go into great detail on the subject of franchising. However, since it may be an option to being self-employed, we do need to at least bring it to your attention. There are three shortcomings that you need to be aware of: 1). The cost of the franchise, 2) the restrictions on growth that may come with a franchising contract, and 3) the loss of absolute independence on the part of the franchise.

If you have an interest in franchising take your time to investigate wisely the franchisor to make sure the business opportunity being offered truly meets your need for the present and the future. The sources of information to get answers to your questions are, the franchisor themselves, government, and trade associations. Talk to other franchisees, they will have valuable input about franchises and also look at business publications. You may also want to speak with a franchise consultant. Like choosing a franchise you need to pick one that is reputable. A franchise consultant is not an attorney so you will want to consult an attorney to review and evaluate all contracts or legal documents before you sign You might want to attend a franchise seminar.

Growth of the Firm

The potential growth and profit of various small business ventures will vary greatly. Some of these ventures will create millionaires, others will provide modest returns to the entrepreneur. Income from some of these small businesses can vary in income from $50,00 to $200,000 annually. In contrast there are firms that provide incomes that will allow the owners barely survive. Recognize that there is an entire range ventures along each point along the spectrum, each of them with varied problems and rewards.  to of

A few firms have such great prospects for growth that they may be called high-potential ventures. You will discover that these firs frequently are high-technology ventures. As a founder you may anticipate rapid growth, a possible merger, or 'go public' within a few years.

The point of this chapter is to suggest that developing your own business is one opportunity to consider as you continue seeking ways to advance your career. In addition, as a small business owner, the rewards can range from just getting by to creating a multi-million dollar enterprise.

CHAPTER TWELVE

The Newsletter

The newsletter as a job search tool can be used effectively. Over the past three years or so, we have mailed out a newsletter, a cover letter, and resume with mixed reviews. We have received calls from presidents of companies that liked this job search tool. We have to say that we got several interviews as a result of sending it out.

The newsletter has been constantly refined and upgraded over this period. It is designed as a supplement to the resume. The newsletter incorporates a combination of things such as goals, achievements, and experiences. It also serves to show computer competency. In addition, the newsletter takes on a unique twist in that it has been used in marketing ideas to get attention.

In your newsletter, should you decide to develop one, you can tailor the content around your expertise and experience. Your letter should reflect you. It will catch the eye of 'key' individuals within a firm offering an alternate device to evaluate and generate an interview. We believe that the design speaks for itself. You can use this concept if you want to. What we say is that it has worked and that not many other appli- cants know this technique and few still have tried the approach. You should <u>not</u> substi- tute the newsletter for a cover letter or resume.

Will it work for you? we cannot say, however, it has worked for us. We us color as well as black and white print. We find the color is the most productive but it is expensive. The cost is about $1.00 a page. So the rule of thumb here is this: If we really want to impress someone, a corporation, school district, or government agency, we mail them a color copy on first class paper. If it is a good job, but not a 'super' one we send black and white copies.

You may send out a copy of the newsletter that you made up yourself. You should update the newsletter as you would your resume. A copy of my newsletter will be exhibited later in this book. I have to admit that the jury is still out as to the total value of this document. However, you may use it to sell some of your special interests, successes, and achievements that don't show up on your resume or in your cover letter.

You may believe that the more information a decision maker has with regard to your experience and attitude, the better the chances. It may or may not be of value. However, this is not always agreed with in the job seeking community. The fact remains that there are many opinions as to what to send and what not to send.

You would prefer to send the color version to everyone. You do not have to be a 'rocket scientist' to work out the numbers as to the financial feasibility. You want to send your best stuff to your best prospects. You want to mine gold in the best gold streams using the best tools you have available to you.

You may have gotten feedback from presidents of several companies that stated they were impressed with your newsletter. Try to get some feedback. You may get some positive feedback but not necessarily a job or an interview. This may not be a defeat if you learn something.

Another side to the newsletter-it does computer experience and aptitude. sured today that being computer liter- nerstone to almost everyone job you for. The date, you may have sent out letters. These documents work for you the state of the job market. Currently, job information indicates ment rate in some areas of the Mid- low. Whereas the unemployment rate states, most specifically California is search results will be different. You suggest as well as use this component you are convinced of its value one way demonstrate your You can be as- ate may be the cor- may want to apply thousands of news- depending upon that the unemploy- west and East is in the Western higher your job should continue to for job search until or another.

If many companies want you to send a history of the salaries you have received from other companies you have worked for, you should include this information. There have been times that you would have preferred not to include this

this document however, some companies state that they will not review your employment package unless this document is present.

Many people today have home a computer. Everyday, more and more companies are requesting that we FAX or E-mail our resumes, cover letter and other related employment documents. It is at times difficult to determine if your FAX was received. Based on my experience (and the advice of several others) when you are FAXing your newsletter use a free-standing FAX machine unless you are totally confident that your FAX modem works perfectly. Follow-up (where possible) with a copy by mail. Sometimes there is no street address to mail your copy to. If you are sending a newsletter an original will show much better for you than a FAX'd copy.

You may place a 'post-it' note inside each newsletter. Here is another 'guerilla' marketing technique. This is an idea as seen in some direct marketing advertising that this author has received. It is suggested that with this technique, the comment or idea will be read and paid more attention. On the 'post-it' note you can write in red, 'Call Me', 'Let's get together,' 'Let's Talk,' etc. You can probably think of other 'Call for Action' sayings on your own that would be appropriate for your newsletter. You will have to try this technique and test it for yourself.

Another idea that can get action from your cover letter is to use a P.S.. The P.S. at the end of your cover letter will get read. Knowing this, we want o put something that is interesting and calls for action on the part of the individual reading your letter. Use this technique wisely as it can overplay your hand.

CHAPTER THIRTEEN

Networking

Today, and perhaps forever, Networking has been the best way by far to get a job or at least to get a favorable interview. You must get in front of the 'herds' of other applications that are out there for every job. There are several types, levels, or categories of networking. It is safe to say that seventy – five to eighty-five percent of jobs are gotten this way. Most jobs are given out by work-of-mouth only. Some employers will ask their employees if they know someone like them that is looking for employment. This is considered the best way to get a job. An employer may go to the outside if there are no candidates for an available position. This process is done in large and small companies as well as government agencies. Most jobs are filled before the positions are posted. Employees will find the people (their friends) to fill an open job if they can.

So, what is the best type of networking? The best, of course, is to have someone who knows personally of your abilities and experience to make direct contact on your behalf. We will call this type of networking 'Net 1.' Any networking is better than no networking! You should try to keep in contact with your network (the person or persons who are assisting in your job search). You do not want to lose what may be an important contact, you may need them later. You should keep in touch at least once a year. People forget who you are if they do not hear from you for a long time. Do not allow this to happen to you. Keep in close contact.

Example:

I, Gene Merhish, called a friend of mine that I have known and worked with for nearly four years. He was a sales representative in the same company for which I worked. His father owned fifty percent of the firm at that time. When I was with the company it was a five million dollar company in the compressed air industry. Today, he is the president, and his father owns the company. Their company has grown into a twelve million dollar major compressed air distributors in California. During the time I was employed with this company, I was the top salesperson for several years in a row. I had an opportunity to have lunch with my old friend, (now president) and current sales manager. We discussed old times and I mentioned the fact that I had been 'downsized' from my most recent sales manager position, and was looking for employment.

My friend stated that when his company placed ads for staffing he gets from 100 - 150 responses. After discussing the challenges of getting a job and it being a tough job market my friend says that he has a business acquaintance that was looking for a regional sales manager for Southern California. It was suggested that I contact his acquaintance at the other company to which I responded it would be much better if he contacted this 'key' person on my behalf. I explained to my friend that his personal recommendation would have more weight then mine and would place me in a better light with the company. I was very familiar with the company, it's business and product line, as I had worked for this company twenty years ago. I provided my business card to my friend who said he would call me the following week.

You should always have a business card to hand out at any meeting you never know who you will run into, or who that person may know. As an alternative, get yourself some 3 x 5 cards. You can write down names and phone numbers of people you meet or provide your name and number if you do not have business cards.

Networking can be used offensively or defensively. <u>Offensively</u>, when you are attempting to use your contacts to assist you in getting a job or interview. You will be asking your 'network' to assist you in finding leads to job opportunities or better yet, suggesting to an employer that they have a friend who would perhaps fit the job opportunity. <u>Defensively</u>, Your 'network' may call and let you know of a rumor about major changes at your company which may involve lay-offs. This advance notice can be great for you as it gives you time to get your resume out on the street. It would be wise to try to confirm this information if at all possible.

I, Robert Dussman, was told while employed by an aerospace company, that in three weeks everyone in my organization who was male, over 40 years old and making over forty thousand dollars a year, was to be laid-off. I told my 'networking' contact that this was illegal and discriminatory and that I doubted that this would happen at the large company for which I worked. Sure enough. /three weeks later, all the people who were male, over 40 years old and making over forty thousand dollars a year were called in for a 'special meeting.' I know what was afoot but could not say anything. The boss 'announced' that we were all being given notice and were to be laid off.

110

One person later sued and got six million dollars in an out-of-court settlement. My 'networking' contact had also called this person.

Networking is critical to your success in any job search. The more people you know the more networking you can do. Remember: NETWORK NETWORK NETWORK. The people you know are your number one asset. Make sure you start here first.

Before you start calling everyone, it is important that you plan your personal contact carefully. Before you go for the phone try to think of everyone you know who might be worth while contacting. Only after you have identified the people you might call, can you determine whom you should call and in what order.

If you know the Chief Executive , president, or owner of a company in the industry you would most like to work for, this should be the number one priority and contact. This person in all likelihood controls at least one job and it could be the one you want. If you met someone at an Industrial Show a few years ago they will probably not remember you. If this is the case then you had better get a new introduction. You may want to write them a letter as you would an important stranger.

Now, if you know a first-class former subordinate who was always considered a genius, 'go-getter' or a dynamic individual and who now is a department manager, Chief engineer, or owns a small business in your industry of interest they might also be a high-priority contact. There may not be a spot in his/her organization for you but he may know someone in your field. Caution, be sure that any of your network contacts have a positive opinion of you, are enthusiastic about you and eager to help. Also be sure that the contact is intelligent, respected, discreet and not a negative person that would potentially tarnish your image simply by affiliation with them.

Be careful, avoid the tendency we all have, to get in touch with the people we know best and are most comfortable with, rather than the one who can do us the most good. You can make the relevant contacts enthusiastic, but it is difficult to make the enthusiastic contact relevant. Make sure you allocate your time accordingly, as we have said, you have only eight hours in the ay to do the job search, make the best of your time.

Levels of Relevance

1. **Power people** These are the persons that can hire you, or have influence in getting you into the position in which you are interested.

2. **Advantage Position** Not the same level as above, but still a valuable contact. These people can be your 'spy in the sky,' your extra eyes and ears. They could be middle management people in companies or organizations that you are interested in. They could be in your field, i.e. teachers, suppliers, parents, administrators, engineers, etc.

3. **No Power nor Advantage** This is the lowest level of relevance and are probably the people outside of your field altogether. Some may be widely connected and you may be interested in their 'bird-dogging' or off-the-wall ideas and suggestions. These are low priority, but occasionally come up with something that could be very useful.

Now you must ask yourself some questions before you use each one of these resources. How well and how favorably does the contact know your achievements and how well does he/she like you personally?

Enthusiastic and Knowledgeable Contact

The next level of contact is the one who is enthusiastic and knowledgeable. They might fall into the following categories:

1. **Co-worker** Your former supervisor, associate principal, subordinate, or your peers. In most cases it is most necessary to sell them, just update them about what you are cur rently doing and what you are trying to achieve, in most cases they will automatically become enthusiastic. However, if they are negative and not excited for you do not even bother with this person. Years ago when Mr. Merhish left Proctor and Gamble his co-worker was very negative about him leaving the company and was so hostile that he called him a quitter. There was nothing that could be said or done to change the co-workers thinking. Just walk away from this person and carry on.

2. **Contacts by Reputation** People you may not know but who have heard and you and your reputation. You may have been involved in a trade association, with competitors, other educators in your field, trade magazines, etc. People that you have met at industry functions, suppliers who have solicited you as a customer, school conferences, and customers that you have solicited. In this situation there is a little more going for you than if the person was a stranger, but not much.

3. **The non-business contact** These are the people on the street or the people you know very well but that are not in your circle of friends. They may be 'long shots' but that may be the shot you are looking for.

SCORE THE CONTACT

Since 'time is money' and the longer you are out of work the more it is costing you, it is important that you develop a scoring system for your contacts. The point of the scoring is to make sure that you spend your valuable time with the contacts that are most likely to be Helpful. It might be easier to spend time with you whose company you enjoy, that is understandable, but these people may not be as beneficial to the advancement of your career. You may use '10' as being the most valuable contact and '1'' the least valuable. It is hoped that this scoring system will keep you on your job seeking target.

After you have completely depleted your ideal business contacts you may want to try a few selective social contacts. You will need to use good judgment in your selection. Make sure that you neglect the ones that are least likely to help you and pursue the ones that are most productive.

In job-hunting it is very important that you keep up-to-date on what is going on in your industry of interest. You cannot get this information if you confine yourself to a desk. Only a few of the people you meet will can give you suitable and valuable career information that you would really find useful. Be careful, and remember, Networking is your #1 winning job search tool. Use it wisely and to your best advantage.

Pursue your contacts in such a way that they remain an asset and do not become a liability. Do not be overly pushy or aggressive or your networking may backfire on you. It must be obvious to you that you do not want to portray yourself in a negative light. You will also not want your contacts making calls to people disclaiming their connection with you. Always assure your contacts and friends that when you use their name that you will never use it inappropriately.

CHAPTER FOURTEEN

The Champion

It can easily be said that today is like no other time in history when it comes to job search. I believe this to be true. We are told that the United States has the lowest level of unemployment in history, but at the same time, we are aware of the fact that there are over five million Americans being put out of work through 'downsizing.' We have identified that it is necessary to send out more than 1,000 resumes before we can realize any interest. We will be fortunate to see 3 - 5 interested parties and perhaps get one interview.

It is difficult and there are times that you will find that you cannot do it without help. You could turn to your 'champion' for help. A champion can do things you cannot do. Should there be a reason why you need to conduct a job search anonymously (perhaps you are employed and want to keep this search confidential for now), your ';champion could help. You could send your anonymous resume out yourself with responses being sent to a post office box. You would need to explain the reason for your secrecy in your cover letter. This approach has been used many times unsuccessfully. In today's busy market no one has time to deal with this type of individual, especially when receiving hundreds of responses to their vacancy.

The 'Champion' is a real live respectable person who can openly send your name-omitted resume and state why he/she is doing so. The 'champion' can also have any responses sent to him/her. It is a big help if the 'champion is known in the industry, someone who would know a qualified individual when they came across one. It will more than likely enhance your image.

'Who can I get to do this for me?' We can safely say it cannot be the President, or bill Gates, Lee Iacocca, or Captain Kangaroo. There is no question that these people are well known and prominent in their own right. They may or may not know who would make an ideal employee in a specific industry. A business acquaintance can become a 'champion' on your behalf. Getting the help of an individual like this should not be beyond your reach. Enlist someone who could begin his/her letter with a good deal of credibility: "As the president of a six million dollar stamping company, I know the importance of having employees that I can count on".

Your 'champion' should have some first-hand knowledge of your outstanding on-the-job performance. He/she should be a former employer, boss, subordinate. We believe that if you have a customer that is keenly aware of your skills, they might make a good 'champion'. You may be able to enlist a prominent business person you know socially or a member of a non-profit institution you may know. We can think of several presidents and production managers of firms that we have had extensive business dealing with as well as several educators in the education community that could also qualify as a 'champion'. You probably have similar contacts. Use them.

You will want to be careful nor to select a too powerful individual within a corporation. The reason for this is that the information in the letter must be believable. It has to sound reasonable as to why they cannot use you in their own organization. A president or executive of a major national or international company would have a hard time explaining why they cannot find a sot for you within their own operation. They may not have any jobs at this time. This will need to be addressed up front.

Important Elements of a 'Champion's" Letter Sent On Your Behalf

1. The champion's credentials must make him/her a valid judge of your skills and abilities.
2. The individual must have a vantage point that enables him/her to evaluate and endorse your on-the-job performance.
3. The recommendation is critical.
4. There must be a believable reason as to why your champion cannot hire you.
5. Justify the reason for secrecy if you send an anonymous version of your resume.
6. There has to be a commitment to you by your champion to keep in touch with the interested party.

The Endorsement

The advantage of the 'Champion' endorsement allows him/her to say positive things about you that you cannot say about yourself. This type introduction is far more believable

Coming from someone else, especially coming from your boss or a senior individual. If it comes from a headhunter, it is less believable since there is a compensation attached to the endorsement.

In some situations, the 'Champion's' direct mail promotion may be the only method to resolve a highly sensitive problem. This approach becomes a highly persuasive marketing process when done well. The endorsement provides a great cover and at the same time it heightens your introduction and problem solving. The Champion's letter should always tell the prospective employer why you would be a great employee. The letter should close with a statement such as, "Please call me at (phone number) if you have any questions. I highly recommend you hire (your name here.)

CHAPTER FIFTEEN

Cold Call Job Search

In an earlier section, we touched on "Cold Calling" on potential employers. This job search technique is not recommended. It takes a lot of time and can be very expensive. Generally, most of the businesses you cold call do not have a job for you when you call on them. The biggest problem with cold calls is that it can be very discouraging, Take a friend to ride along with you if you decide you would like to do this. You will find there is less than one opportunity  for every 1,000 organizations you call on. Your friend may be able to keep your spirits ups. If you are an hourly worker, you may find this more effective, but again you will have to call on a good many firms before you find an open position for your trade, or expertise. It would be a good idea if you opt to try this approach to take along a good number of resumes, and your business cards.

It is also im-possible to talk to "key" executives because of the "gatekeeper". The gate keeper, as you may know, is the secretary or receptionist. They have been instructed to keep job seekers and other disruptions away from the executives so that they can deal with corporation responsibilities. So most of the time, you only get to talk to the secretary or receptionist. In many cases, these gatekeepers do not know of any openings or are instructed not to reveal this information. The gatekeeper is only instructed to take resumes and/or application and forward them to the Human Resources Department. You may try to get a shot at seeing the Personal Department or Human Resources. In many cases they may be aware of job postings. In the Education arena, and in Government you will find flyers and circulars of job openings. Since these are public employment agency they are available for your viewing. Be aware of the fact that positions that are being posted are time active and have predetermined closing dates.

You may want to talk to colleagues and friends and if the best you can come up with is cold calling I would suggest that you to it in teams. The entire exercise is extremely frustrating, and in most cases there is little benefit. Cold calling on organizations is not for the faint of heart and is not recommended.

There are a few successful businesses that require their sales force to do 'cold calling' but these companies are becoming fewer and fewer as time goes on. The professional salesman recognizes the importance of prospecting, planning, having a strong opening, an outstanding presentation, the importance of building good will, and being able to close the deal. He also recognizes the need for maximizing time management. Do not forget for a moment that you must be a salesman in your job search and that the most important product you have to offer is you.

We cannot tell you not to make cold calls, we can only point out that this is a very time consuming process and that generally there is a low rate of return. But, like any other job search method, it is a numbers game. We do not want to see you spending valuable time and money 'racing around' your community 'ringing doorbells' and being 'shot down' by the gatekeeper before you even get started.

Remember, in job search, it is important to pick the best techniques and strategies for you and that have worked particularly well for job seekers in the past.

CHAPTER SIXTEEN

Headhunters

Professional 'headhunters' may work for you. They can cost over $3,000. This is before they even get started. There is no guarantee of a job at the end. There are also headhunters that advertise themselves as 'free.' The paid consultant or management search firms are painted as being able to find you a better and higher paying position. You should not dispute this but you may have less than satisfactory experiences with them. Generally, they will do anything to get you to sign up for their services and many times they do very little thereafter.

There are several types of headhunters and in my opinion, are basically not your friend. We are not going to tell you not to use them however. They can be valuable. You may have good luck with them. We will admit that there were times in our careers that we did advance our employment situation by using man-  agement search firms. You may find that it is important to understand how they work for you or against you. You will also want to know how they work for the employer and them- selves. Headhunters may be offering services as an em- ployment consultant, contingency employment, employ- ment agency, retainer recruiter, management re- cruiter, etc. You should look closely at each one of these and de- termine if they can be beneficial to you.

If you are introduced to an employer by a search — firm, you come with a price tag on your head. This price tag can be tens of thousands of dollars depending on the position being recruited for. If you come to the employer on your own, you will not have this price tag and the employer may overlook a particular skill you are lacking but can be taught if overall you are the type of candidate he had in mind and the large fee will be saved. With the price tag route the employer will want every skill or ex- perience covered.

Some employers, because of the volume of work they do with an agency, pay a retainer so it is safe to assume that this headhunter is going to present applicants that meet every criteria. The fact is, if you do not have all that the employer is looking for you are not going to be presented. If you are being presented, during this consideration process you will not be presented to any other employer until the first headhunter is done with you and you are back in the file.

The contingency headhunter might present you but he is also going to present other applicants. The contingency headhunter does not get paid unless the employer selects one of his applicants. Consequently, his loyalty to you as a client is slim to none.

We discussed the job consultant that you paid up to $3,000 or more for their service. This type of headhunter will help you with your application, letters of introduction, even distribution of your resume. These paid consultants will help you learn terms and refresh you on your interviewing techniques and skills. You must be careful in your selection, as well as you must be able to afford this service. Be aware of the fact that they cannot and will not guarantee that they will get you a job.

I had a personal experience with this type of headhunter, which resulted in my having to forfeit $1,500 to the consultant. Although I had started interacting with the consultant I managed to find a sales management position on my own. . I was unable to get any of my money back from the consultant even though the firm was only in the beginning phase of my file. I did like some of the stuff that the agency could do for me but was it worth the money, more than likely not.

There is nothing that these firms can tell you to do that you cannot do for yourself with the help of this book. They can be a waste of your time and money if you are of the opinion that they can guarantee you employment. As we indicated, these agencies cannot guarantee you employment. They are perhaps a fraction of the amount of monies you may pay them. Time is the problem. You may not be able to wait for them to perform. If time and money is not an issue for you this may be a viable resource You should plan for over a month, or two, perhaps longer, if you plan to have this resource work for you. Keep in mind it may never work.

One of the things that we have discovered in regard to 'free headhunters' is that if you are somewhat hard to place or you do not fit any of their openings quickly, they will drop you. The contingency headhunter may be broadcasting your resume without first letting you know where they have been sent. Should you, as an individual, approach one of these companies, you will have a 'price tag on your head' which may put you out of the running before you have a chance to present your special skills and talents.

Most headhunters will ask you to list every company that you have contacted. He will not want to waste time going to a company that you have already approached. Be sure to keep your list updated.

We can understand you may feel compelled to contact a headhunter for help out of frustration. You may be setting yourself up for trouble. You are now in the right position for the contingency recruiter to put that price tag on your head and rush your resume to potential employers before you do. And at the same time, you are equally vulnerable to have the same price tag applied by a retainer recruiter. So now it is possible for you to wind up with a double price on your head.

You cannot tell when you are going to obtain the services of a recruiter, what type of recruiter you are getting as there is not a door sign indicating their type of business. The recruiter can also change roles from time to time. It will be very important for you to discuss the type of business this agency has and how you will fit into the picture.

It is only natural, when present yourself to the recruiter, you want to present yourself in the most favorable manner. The problem here is that the contingency recruiter is inclined to 'blast' your resume everywhere. He wants people lots of people coming in as the more 'bread upon the water' the better chance for him/her to make money. So if your appointment is easy to get and if you are rushed through the interview favorably, your warning bell and lights should go off in your head. You are probably working with a recruiter that sees you as the next highly marketable 'meal ticket.'

Be wary of the recruiter who tells you only what you want to hear. You do not want to be circulated unless the recruiter takes the time to get your approval to submit your resume, etc. to a firm or organization.

CHAPTER SEVENTEEN

The Cover Letter

Perhaps one of the most important documents you will send to a potential employer, if not the most important, is the Cover Letter. The Cover Letter is the very first thing that the employer will see. It may be the only thing that he or she will see. You have just a few seconds to gain interest which can make the difference as to whether or not you will get an interview. The cover letter is your introduction to the specific person who may be hiring you. Remember, the average employer will spend only 10-15 seconds in your cover letter and about the same amount of time on your resume. You must hit them fast or you will miss the opportunity. You will not get the job if your resume is in the trash can!

The contents of the cover letter should tell the employer that you have knowledge of the company or organization and that you are qualified to meet the challenge of the position for which you are applying. It is also to your advantage to mention that you are a team player even though you may need to work independently.

As your cover letter grabs the interest of the reader, it will need to cover areas about your and your qualifications that are not directly included in your resume. It is our opinion that the cover letter is an excellent spot to sell the special things that you can bring to the employer as well as review character strengths and attributes. This is where you toot your horn.

We hope that we do not have to tell you this, however, a reminder never hurts, handwritten letters and resumes are not appropriate. Your letter should be typed and by all means make sure the grammar is perfect and your spelling is without error. A word about copies. Do not mail self made cheap appearing copies. This can be interpreted as insincere and lacking true interest. First quality copies can be made at your local copying business (Kinko's, Copy Max, Office Depot). It is crucial that you always present your <u>very best effort</u> every time you send a letter and resume.

All cover letters should be on 8-1/2" x 11" white or light colored bond paper. Whatever you do, make sure that you get the name of the person and his/her title spelled correctly. Sending letters to Whom It May Concern, Dear Sir, Gentlemen or Madam have little change of reaching anyone except the wastebasket. You will probably be wasting your time. If you are answering a blind ad the name of the individual may not be provided. The best can do in this situation is to address the cover letter to the department, etc that is indicated in the ad.

Develop your resume first then your cover letter. Make sure that you are selling yourself with everything that you have. In many cases, you may be in competition with up to 100 or more people with every ad you respond to. You will want to prepare a new cover letter that directly responds to every position you respond to.

In the last paragraph of your letter, state that you will be contacting the company or organization on a specific day if you do not hear from them. You want them to know that their company and their position are the most important priorities for you. Also, include your phone number and the times that you can be reached.

Structure Points

1. Make sure your grammar and spelling are correct.

2. Keep the cover letter on one page if at all possible but do not sell yourself short. Use two pages if necessary, as long as it is as concise as possible.

3. Avoid 'bold; or 'fancy' paper. Use 8-1/2" x 11" bond. White, light blue, light gray, buff and ivory are acceptable. No dark paper incase copies are made. Paper weigh between 16-25 lbs is neither too thin or too thick and presents well for this purpose. paper texture can be linen finish or rag paper the choice is your personal decision.

4. Avoid using the personal pronoun 'I' whenever possible. Simply leave it out of each sentence if at all possible.

5. Use a layout that has good spacing, margins and headings. A little creativity can shout 'Read Me." Experiment with your page design until you are confident that you have an 'eye catching' format.

Word Processing Service

Many of us are not competent behind the typewriter or computer. If this is your case you You will want to hire a professional typist or data processing person to prepare your cover letter and resume. You can look in your local newspaper or local yellow pages for persons or businesses that specialize in cover letters and resumes.

One of the nicest features of word processors versus typewriters is that the word processor has the ability to store typed information on a disc. This of course allows checking spelling, grammar, or needed modifications. You will be able to tailor your cover letter and resume to the specific job. This modification process can be done in a matter of minutes.

The sharpest print is obtained from a laser printer which most word processing services generally use. We would suggest that you do not accept type formats known as dot matrix or thermal as this will not offer the sharpness you will want for your letter and resume.

Word processing services come and go. Therefore, you will want to obtain several copies of your letter and resume and also ask for the disc so that another service can modify your paperwork is necessary. Unfortunately, things can happen to discs so you will want to have a copy or two as backups. The most common word processing programs used today are Microsoft 95, 98 or Microsoft Office 2000. These programs will be around for some time and are very popular therefore, you should be able to find more than one word processing service to assist you if necessary.

You will have a superior quality cover letter and resume comparable to those found in books, magazines and newspapers. You can expect to be charged between $25-$75. Insist on a font (print type) that is easy on the eye and is clear. Avoid fancy script. Your cover letter and resume must say BUSINESS DOCUMENT from start to finish.

Font types (print types) the type size for each of the following is #12:

Times New Roman: Easy to read and clear type.

Centaur: Appears like this-a little less clear

Arial: Easy to read and clear type

Select the font that best meets your needs. Most of the time you will be able to see the style that best suits your taste. Once you have decided on a font stick with it. A letter with more than one font type is unattractive to the eye and appears confusing. To liven up the visual impact you can use variations of this font by changing from regular to bold or to italics. You can very the impact of keywords with italics, underlining important phrases, or bold and/or capitalize titles for additional emphasis.

Once your cover letter and resume is completed please take the time to proofread them. The typists are not perfect. Check everything from beginning to end. This is also a perfect time to make any modifications to your paperwork. It never seems to fail that once you see your letter and resume in print that you feel it will look better in a different format or you have forgotten to include something or would like to delete something.

- Is the layout and set-up the way you want it?
- /are all typographic errors corrected?
- Is the punctuation correct?
- How the high-lighted, underlined, capitalized, bolded, italicized and indentations been done appropriately and to your satisfaction.

You may want to have a second person review your cover letter and resume. You will want this person to be objective and catch any errors you may have missed. They should also be able to read for content and assure you that it will be positively received by a prospective employer.

Cover Letter Examples

Take some time and review the examples of cover letters that we are providing you. You too can write dynamite cove letters like these. You can use these cover letters if you would like. However, be sure to modify them to fit your needs specific to the job you are applying for.

Please refer to next page so that the letters can be seen as a whole document and not split up by page changes.

Example #1

Gene Merhish
123 Home Town Road
All America, CA 12345

May 9, 1998

 Personnel Service
Cerritos Community College District
11110 Alondra Blvd.
Norwalk, CA 90650-6298

RE: Full-time/Part-time; Business Education, Advertising, Marketing,
     Retailing, and related courses

Dear Colleague:

A few years ago I taught up to three nights a week for Riverside Community College.
Then as I was informed, my services were deleted due to a down-turn in student enroll-
ment. I am continuing my search for a teaching position at the junior college level.

The intent of this letter is to throw my hat into the ring to let you know of my interest. I
have taught at four (4) junior colleges, six (6) adult education programs and at the univer-
sity and high school levels. In addition, I have twenty-six (26) years of Industrial and
Business experience. I also operated one if the most advanced programs in the teaching of
Distributive Education in the Western States and was appointed as a consultant for the
California Department of Business Education.

I would welcome an opportunity to once again teach full-time or part-time for your Community College. I may be reached at my office at, 310-123-4567, ext 7777 Monday
through Friday or at home, 714-123-4567 after 5:00 p.m.

Sincerely,

Gene Merhish, M.A.

126

Anita Haviland
1234 Blank Road
Riverside, CA 92507

April 5, 1998

Mr. Dick Gregory
Personnel Director
Madness, Inc.
331 Block Drive, Suite 24
Los Angeles, CA 92725

Dear Mr. Gregory:

Ms. Mimi Fashion, manager of Fabulous Fashion Boutique in Riverside, suggested that I get in touch with you. She says you are now staffing three new shops in Los Angeles County, and need experienced, capable, and enthusiastic sales people. I think I qualify for the Madness team.

I have worked for Fabulous Fashions for almost two years, selling and modeling. My familiarity with the Friden stock control system may be especially valuable to you since your new store will be using that equipment. I've been responsible for training all new employees since last November in the Friden system, as well as in selling techniques.

Details of my experience, training, and other qualifications are summarized in the enclosed resume.
May I meet with you personally to answer any questions you may have. You cal call me between 8:00 a.m. and 11:00 a.m. at 714-555-6666. Between the hours of 11:30 a.m. and 8:30 p.m. I can be reached at 714-222-8888.

Sincerely,

Anita Haviland

Example #3:

1500 Main Street, Brea, CA 90638, phone 714-670-0000

(ADDRESSEE)

Dear (Company Name)

I am interested in seeing you about a job.

My objective is to utilize my 12 years as an engineer (and an equal amount of in-depth business experience) to contribute to the one area that has always been the most satisfying for me, manufacturing.

My departure from the engineering field was one of mutual reluctance; I had been a business unit manager and was asked to join the staff at another company. I possess strong people skills so I decided to move on.

I have been an associate engineer, engineer, and engineering manager. I have never lost my love of engineering but I must move on.

Please call me at 714-666-4444 to further discuss how I might be a positive addition to your company. I look forward to hearing from you to further exploring your opportunities.

Yours truly,

Joe Books

Enclosure

Example #4

DIRECT MAKET PENETRATION LETTER

Date

Addressee

Dear_____:

Recently, I have been conducting research to identify (COMPANIES, ORGANIZA-TIONS, FIRMS) to which I thought I could make significant contributions in/as (POSITION, RESPONSIBILITIES, OR TARGET). During the course of this research I identified your (COMPANY, ORGANIZATION, FIRM). I feel that you would want to be aware of my interest and availability as much as I am interested in learning of your needs.

I offer proven background, experience and ability which will provide specific competencies including:

- INSERT KEY CONCEPTS

- OR

- STRENGTHS, ABILITIES, OR TRANSFERABLE SKILLS

I am confident that you will agree that a personal meeting will be of mutual interest and benefit.

While you are reviewing my qualifications, please note that I will contact your office. I will discuss any questions that you have at that time. I am most desirous of setting up an introductory meeting.

I look forward to speaking with you.

Sincerely,

(Note: This is a 'stand alone' letter. Do not enclose or attach anything to this letter.)

Example #5

April 8, 1998

Dear Sir/Madame;

I would appreciate the opportunity to talk to you regarding an employment opportunity with your organization. I am excited about the possibility of applying my education and experience to any position you have available.

I would be happy to provide you with any additional information. I look forward to hearing from you soon.

Sincerely,

Joe The Rag Man
1234 Main Street
Anywhere, USA 90638
714-555-4444

Example #6

REFERENCE 'ACKNOWLEDGMENT' COVER LETTER

Date

Addressee

Dear _____:

I would like to express my thanks for your willingness to permit me to use your name as a reference in my job search campaign. While my campaign gains momentum you will undoubtedly receive calls from potential employers with whom I have been in contact. I felt that it would b helpful for you to have some information available which would highlight my work experience and qualifications. You are familiar with most of my background but I thought it would b helpful if I would attach a current resume so that you have the details on hand.

In addition, I am also enclosing a list of other persons who have agreed to be a reference for me. Many potential employers will ask for additional names of individuals that they may contact. I have sent each one of my references the same information that I am providing for you. You may wish to consider one or more of these names if you are asked for additional references. I appreciate your support and the willingness to help me during my job search.

Please contact me when there is activity from a potential employer. I will be contacting you periodically to keep you advised of my progress.

Sincerely,

Enclosures: resume
               reference list

Example #7

DIRECT MARKET 'NO TIME TO RESEARCH' COVER LETTER
(fastest way into the job market but less effective than example #4 letter)

Date

Addressee

Dear _____: (contact name and/or title goes on the envelope only)

I am using this informal but personal note to contact you as I wanted to get my resume into your hands quickly.

Recently I have been conducting research on (COMPANIES, ORGANIZATIONS, FIRMS) in your industry. I have identified yours as one to which I feel I can make a significant contribution in a position that is key to your activities in:

(INSERT POSITION, RESPONSIBILITY OR TARGET)

Therefore, I am letting you know of my interest, experience, and availability. As you review my profile, I am sure it will stimulate your thinking as to areas in your organization that would profit through my (TECHNICAL, MANAGEMENT) skills.

While you still have my profile in hand and its contents in mind, why don't you give me a telephone call. I will be happy to discuss any concerns or answer any questions. We can also explore the desirability of an initial introductory meeting.

I look forward to hearing from you in the near future.

Sincerely

Enclosure: resume

Example #8

(Cover letter to market yourself to an employment agency, search firm, or recruiter)

Date

Addressee

Dear Recruiter:

The enclosed profile should be of interest to you as you review your client assignments. My outstanding background will assist you when selecting an individual for opportunities in the areas of:

(INSERT: POSITION, RESPONSIBILITY, OR TARGET)

Please, take just a moment while you still have my documents before you and give me a call. We can set up an exploratory meeting convenient to your schedule. At that time I will also be happy to answer any questions concerning my background and experiences.

I look forward to hearing from you.

Sincerely,

Enclosure: resume

Example #9

(cover letter for answering ads or blind p.p. Boxes)

Date

Addressee

Dear Advertiser:

I feel that my profiler is one that you will want to review in detail. It appears that I have all of the qualifications mentioned in your advertised position:

(MENTION QUALIFICATIONS/SKILLS THAT WERE IN THE AD)

I am looking forward to hearing from you to answer any questions or clarifying any issue you may have. I can be reached at 714-555-6666. We can also explore the feasibility of setting up an introductory meeting.

Sincerely,

Enclosure: resume

Example #9

(re-activation or follow-up letter)

Date

Addressee

Dear _____:

I am following up my earlier letter to you suggesting that we get together to discuss the way in which my experience, knowledge and skills could be combined to benefit your organization. I continue to be very much interested in your (COMPANY, ORGANIZATION, FIRM) and possible opportunities where my abilities would increase your sales/revenue and/or reduce your costs, expenses and overhead while increasing your profits.

Included in the personal profile of a successful (RESUME POSITION) is a reluctance to give up easily. It is for that reason that I am contacting you again.

(CHOOSE ONE OF THE FOLLOWING)

A. Not having heard from you, I wanted to follow-up as every professional must, to be certain that no worthwhile opportunity has been missed.

B. I am disappointed that your response was not more encouraging. Perhaps a number of considerations prevent a positive reaction at this time. There may be someone else however, who might be able to review my credentials. I would appreciate that opportunity.

I believe strongly that my talents, transferable skills and capabilities are relevant and that I would make an immediate and profitable contribution to your firm. Please take a moment To review the enclosed accomplishments and results overview.

(CHOOSE ONE OF THE FOLLOWING)

A. While you have this letter in hand, why not call at (Phone number).
B. As a follow up to this letter, I will plan on calling you.

I will be happy to clarify any issues you may have or answer any questions. We can also discuss a mutually convenient meeting.

Sincerely,

Chapter Eighteen
The Resume

What we would like to do here is to review several types of resumes, the Functional Resume, the Combination or Eclectic Resume, etc. You must keep in mind results count when it comes to resumes. The one that gets you the job is the best. Everyone that you talk to will tell you that their design is the best or works. Your resume fails if you do not get the job.

Whether you should keep a ple hire peo- influence one and under- design your sume, you functions and not least, say use the samples that we provide or develop your own, you few things in mind. First, companis do not hire people. People; therefore, when you prepare a resume, the purpose is to or more people. Often, through research, you can develop stand these people's needs, wants, and desires, so you can resume around this information. When you prepare your resume should provide your objectives, after you have learned the objectives of the specific job you hope to obtain. Last but nothing you can't back up. Don't lie. If you do, this very well will cost you the job. The employer may check up on every word you say.

The Chronological Resume

The most widely used resume is the Chronological, and it is traditionally accepted. Most employers are accustomed to seeing a resume of this type. Counselors consider the chronological resume the only acceptable format to be presented. However, we do not believe that there is 1 "one" typr of anything. And just because some counselors voice their opinions does not make it gospel. Would you see one doctor if you needed major surgery and only take his word? This may not be life or death, but it might be. What we would recommend is that you present your assets and qlualifications in the format that best sells your skills.

Your resume must fit you. You will be the one defending it. When your employment history shows a graduating progression of jobs in the same career field for which you are educationally prepared, the best format may be the Chronological Resumes.

If the Chronological Resume is your decision, developing this format and content is simple. You list your work history and educational history in reverse chronological order, putting the most recent first. What employers what to see is not only what you did but how well you performed the task. In other words, "I increased te sales by 20 percent," ir " I was able to reduce expenses and improved the bottom line for the company." Use numbers to show what you did. Brag about your accomplishments. When developing your resume, review your strengths and versatility; use statements that detail the depth of your skills and responsibilities you took on. Most importantly, spell out your most notable accomplishment in each position that you held.

Note: you will find examples of resumes included within this book.

The Functional Resume

The Functional Resume concentrates on your job skills, abilities, qualification, and what you have done under individual headings which are related to your objectives. If you have gotten information about the specific job you are applying for, your resume will include those accomplishments and objectives that correspond to the functions of the job you are applying for.

Even though the Functional Resume format does not speak to your work history or the lack of work history, it is an excellent way of presenting information that corresponds to the requirements of the job you are seeking. Use numbers to highlight accomplishments.

Without knowing the specifics of the jobs you are going after, it is some-what difficult to construct a Functional Resume. If, however, you can get good job description of the position you want, it will be Easier to develop.

Combination Resume

This resume has elements from the other resumes. Generally it does not have an occupational goal stated. This information is given in a cover letter.

Advantage of the Combination Resume:

1. May be personalized
2. Hits goals achieved
3. Makes a point quickly

Disadvantages of the Combination Resume:

1. No standard way of doing it
2. It may not be recognized as a resume
3. Some people have not seen it before
4. You must have strong work skills to use

The Tailor-Made Resume

During your job search, drafting a resume and cover letter in response to a newspaper want ad will be required.

You will want to write down on a piece of paper each function that is required and each requirement. Study the ad carefully. You will next want to write down your experience and skills that you have that are transferable or correspond. You will need to organize your skills in the most positive terms so that you do not miss any important details. Next, de- velop your re- sume. Once this is completed, develop your cover letter. By developing your resume and cover letter in this fashion, you will have carefully arranged your skills and ex- perience in the best possible light to coincide with the requirements of the want ad.

You must hit the target immediately. You will not ever get another chance with this employer. Your points must be made quickly and correctly. You must gather the reader's interest right away.

Other Resumes

As were saying earlier, any combination of the parts of a resume you can put together to create a unique and effective resume is fair game in getting that job. If you want to combine components of the Functional Resume with that of the Chronological Resume, go ahead. Our advice is that you maintain a log of what type of resume you are sending and to whom. This information can be valu- able for future resume development. If you want to develop a Combination Resume and cover letter, give it a try. But knowing the recipient will help in your development.

We can assure you that the resume that shows the most originality will get the most action. So many resumes look the same that they a "blur" looking as if they came from the same resume mill. If, from your research, you have determined that you are the ideal person for the job, you owe it to yourself to break away from the traditional and be a little creative. But bear in mind, if you find out that recipi- ent of your resume is a conservative person, you may want to approach this induvidual with a more traditional format.

Note: Examples of other resumes will be included in these pages.

Any resume may be limited to about one page. Some employers will not look at a resume longer than a page. You may use more if you have a long job history. Remember, an employer will not spend a lot of time on your resume. An employer may spend even less time if he/she feels that he/ she will have to do a lot of work to find out about you.

You should always make it as easy as possible for the employer. Remember, this is the person you want to sell yourself to. Be careful.

A resume is just a thumbnail sketch of you. All the details can be filled in later at your interview. You must grab the reader's attention quickly. You must hold the reader's attention until he/she decides that he/she likes you and wants to interview you.

An employer will move heaven and earth of he/she decides he/she likes you. An employer may do nothing for you (even though you are qualified) if he/she does not like you. Opinions are hard to change once set. Try to get the reader to like you. It is important to you.

You can do this in a number of ways You should he very clear on want you are saying. Do not use abbreviations. They may con-fuse the reader. Use short, clear information on the resume. Make your resume something that you would like to read. Re-member, a busy employer will look at hundreds of resumes every day. Try to make yours one that the reader will remember. Make your resume stand out from the others for the same posi-tion. Show them you have what they want.

CHRONOLOGICAL RESUME

Robert A. Dussman
123 Main Street, La Mirada, CA   90638
Phone (714) 670-7818

Objective:
CONTRACTS MANAGER, and/or BUYER,
PURCHASING MANAGER, MATERIAL and
PROCUREMENT MANAGER.

JOB LEVELS
1. -BROKER/TEACHER, Employee Benefits Contracts, 7 Years, NA
2. -DOUGLAS, Administrator for Purchasing of Aircraft Parts and Systems,   Specification Control and Compliance, 7 years, 65K
3. -NORTHROP, Contracts Manager of Aircraft Systems, 3 Years, 55K
4. -BOEING, Administrator of Procurement of Aircraft Parts, 2 Years, 18K
5. -SEATTLE FIRST BANK, Development and Purchasing, 2 Years, 15K
6. -U.S. NAVY, Procurement Administration, 5 Years, 15K

EXPERIENCE
* Contracts Manager with knowledge of FAR, TINA, etc.
* Negotiated customer changes and implementation of those changes
* Team leader for changes and implementation of changes including pricing
* Experienced in various areas such as engineering, quality control, manufacturing, etc.
* Wrote area procedures for cost, schedule and contract performance
* Preparation of various types of management reports
* Familiar with different types of proposals and requests for proposals
* Preparation of detailed reports before and after negotiations including proposals and their
   supporting packages
* Negotiated and implemented cost reduction efforts for customer
* Experienced with commercial and government contracts

* Responsible for some types of cost estimates including cost/price skills
* Procurement and sub contracts ranging from construction to health packages
* Familiar with contracts close outs
SALARY REQUIREMENTS: OPEN

EDUCATION
Diploma--Computers and Networking--Santa Fe Technical College
BA degree--UNIVERSITY OF OKLAHOMA
MBA degree--NATIONAL UNIVERSITY
JD degree--PACIFIC COAST UNIVERSITY

References Available on Request

CHRONOLOGICAL RESUME

ROBERT DUSSMAN
123 Main Street
La Mirada, CA 90638   Phone (714) 670-7819

OBJECTIVE: TEACHER (SEEKING A PERMANENT POSITION WITH AN
EMERGENCY CREDENTIAL).
TEACHING EXPERIENCE: SUBSTITUTE TEACHER
Anaheim, Whittier Union High, La Mirada/Norwalk and ABC
School District 1995-7
        Provided help to regular teachers for classes,
research, discipline problems, etc. in High School and Grade
Schools to support the District's Objectives. Taken and
passed CBEST Test.

Regular Teacher COMPUTERS FOR BUSINESS VOCATIONAL TRAINING
Centinela Valley High School District, Leuzinger High School
1997--Present
        Provided regular classroom instruction for
computer classes to support the District's Objectives

WORK EXPERIENCE:
    1.-BROKER, Employee Benefits Contracts, 7 Years (1990-
1992 and 1993-   Present)
    2.-DOUGLAS, Contracts and Engineering Administrator, 7
Years (1982-87),   (1992-1993)
    3.-NORTHROP, Contracts and Business Administrator, 3
Years (1987-90)
    4.-BOEING, Administrator, 2 Years (1980-82)
    5.-SEATTLE FIRST BANK, Administrator, 2 Years (1978-80)
    6.-U.S. NAVY, Officer, 5 Years (1973-78)

        Worked on various government and commercial contracts
including contract negotiations, contract awards,
negotiating prices, terms and conditions, delivery, contract
terminations, manufacturing methods, and cost reductions.
Familiar with Business Law.

Education:
* BA DEGREE--History UNIVERSITY OF OKLAHOMA, 1973
* MBA DEGREE--Business NATIONAL UNIVERSITY, 1978
* JD DEGREE--PACIFIC COAST UNIVERSITY, 1988

*   Continued Education Training in - Computer-Electronic
Technician and NetWare 3.12.
*   Took classes for Microsoft Products at Prosoft
*   Knowledgeable of word processing, spread sheets and data
bases
*   Other interests: golf, walking and running

CHRONOLOGICAL RESUME

ROBERT DUSSMAN
123 Main Street
La Mirada, CA 90638   Phone (714) 670-7818

OBJECTIVE:

A position leading to a long term opportunity for the future
        in Manufacturing or Industrial Engineering

Experience:
    1.-VARIOUS PLACES, Stock Broker/Teacher, NA, (1991, 1993
to now)
    2.-DOUGLAS, Manufacturing and Industrial Engineer, 65K,
(1982-87, 1992)
    3.-NORTHROP, Manufacturing and Industrial Engineer in
Contracts, 55K, (1987-90)
    4.-BOEING, Manufacturing and Industrial Engineer in
Development, 25K, (1980-82)
    5.-SEATTLE FIRST BANK, Industrial Engineer in Corporate
Areas, 18K, (1978-80)
    6.-U.S. NAVY, Administration and Methods Engineering, 5
Years, 15K, (1973-78)
FUNCTIONAL EXPERIENCE

* Did methods analysis, work measurement and layouts.
* Cell team leader.
* Familiar with complete projects concepts from cradle to
grave.
* Team manager for changes.
* Responsible for quality projects including TQMS.
* Team leader for proposals.
* Represented and sold proposals to higher levels of
management.
* Familiar with cost reduction initiatives.
* Performed reviews for higher management.
* Wrote area procedures.
* Responsible for facilities projects.
* Responsible for controlling, staffing, directing,
coordination and planning for projects.
* Have experience in most areas including manufacturing,
QA, engineering, facilities,
        logistics, etc.
* Did complete cost analysis for projects including cost
reductions.

Education
*   BA DEGREE-History UNIVERSITY OF OKLAHOMA, 1973
*   MBA DEGREE-Business NATIONAL UNIVERSITY, 1978
*   JD DEGREE-PACIFIC COAST UNIVERSITY, 1988
*   Other-Courses completed for Masters in Public
Administration, University of Northern
    Colorado, 1976. Continued Education Training in
progress - Computer-electronic
    technician and NetWare 3.12.
    Other Interests: golf, walking and running

CHRONOLOGICAL RESUME

ROBERT DUSSMAN
123 Main Street
La Mirada, CA 90638   Phone (714) 670-7817

OBJECTIVE: LAW CLERK

LEGAL EXPERIENCE:

Voluntary Law Clerk, Public Defenders Office North
Court, Fullerton, CA
1990-1991
Provided help to lawyers with Memorandums, Trial
Tactics, Legal   Research, Motions, Computer
Related Work, Legal Briefs, Case Files and   Client
Interviews, etc.

WORK EXPERIENCE:

1.-BROKER, Employee Benefits Contracts, 2 Years (1993-
Present)
2.-DOUGLAS, Contracts and Engineering Administrator, 7
Years (1982-87)
     (1992-1993)
3.-NORTHROP, Contracts and Business Administrator, 3
Years (1987-90)
4.-BOEING, Administrator, 2 Years (1980-82)
5.-SEATTLE FIRST BANK, Administrator, 2 Years (1978-80)
6.-U.S. NAVY, Officer, 5 Years (1973-78)

Worked on various government and commercial contracts
including contract   negotiations, contract awards,
negotiating prices, terms and conditions,   delivery,
contract terminations, manufacturing methods, and cost
              reductions. Familiar with Business Law.

1973-1978 United States Navy Regular Officer

Education:

* BA DEGREE - History UNIVERSITY OF OKLAHOMA, 1973
* MBA DEGREE - Business NATIONAL UNIVERSITY, 1978
* JD DEGREE - PACIFIC COAST UNIVERSITY, 1988

*   Other - Courses completed for Masters in Public
Administration, University of Northern
      Colorado, 1976. Continued Education Training in
progress - Computer-Electronic
      Technician and NetWare 3.12.
*   Familiar with WESTLAW CD-ROM research
*   Knowledgeable of word processing, spread sheets and data
bases
*   Other Interests: golf, walking and running

CHRONOLOGICAL RESUME

                        Robert A. Dussman
                        123 Main Street
                        La Mirada, CA 90638
                        Phone (714) 670-7815

Resume For
      PERSONNEL / ADMINISTRATION

JOB LEVELS
1. BROKER 3 Years
2. DOUGLAS 7 Years
3. NORTHROP 3 Years
4. BOEING 2 Years
5. SEATTLE FIRST BANK 2 Years
6. U.S. NAVY 5 Years

FUNCTIONAL EXPERIENCE
* Did planning, staffing, controlling, coordinating and
directing for various personnel
   projects
* Monitored affirmative action plans
* Monitored eeoc and minority business clauses in contracts
* Team Leader for changes
* Worked with all functional areas
* Wrote area procedures
* Did all types of management reports
* Did incentive programs
* Generated all types of correspondence
* Administered pay and benefit programs
* Negotiated cost reduction efforts
* Worked commercial and government contracts
* Responsible for all types of training

EDUCATION
BA degree-UNIVERSITY OF OKLAHOMA
MBA degree-NATIONAL UNIVERSITY
JD degree-PACIFIC COAST UNIVERSITY
All course work completed for MPA-UNIVERSITY OF NORTHERN
COLORADO

CHRONOLOGICAL RESUME

Robert A. Dussman
123 Main Street
La Mirada, CA 90638
Phone (714) 670-7015

Resume For
     CUSTOMER SERVICE ADMINISTRATOR

JOB LEVELS
1. BROKER 3 Years
2. DOUGLAS 7 Years
3. NORTHROP 3 Years
4. BOEING 2 Years
5. SEATTLE FIRST BANK 2 Years
6. U.S. NAVY 5 Years

FUNCTIONAL EXPERIENCE
* Familiar with all types of customer service
* Familiar with complete customer needs
* Negotiated all types of customer service contracts
* Team Leader for changes
* Worked with all functional areas
* Wrote area procedures
* Did all types of management reports
* Familiar with all types of proposals
* Generated all types of correspondence
* Negotiated customer changes
* Negotiated cost reduction efforts
* Worked commercial and government contracts
* Responsible for all types of cost estimates

EDUCATION
BA degree-UNIVERSITY OF OKLAHOMA
MBA degree-NATIONAL UNIVERSITY
JD degree-PACIFIC COAST UNIVERSITY
All course work completed for MPA-UNIVERSITY OF NORTHERN
COLORADO

CHRONOLOGICAL RESUME

                          Robert A. Dussman
                          123 Main Street
                          La Mirada, CA 90638
                          Phone (714) 777-7080

Objective:

COMPUTER TECHNICIAN / EDP MANAGER

JOB LEVELS
     1. -BROKER, Employee Benefits Contracts, 4 Years
     2.-DOUGLAS, Administrator EDP Manufacturing and
Engineering, 7 Years
     3.-NORTHROP, Administrator EDP Contracts, 3 Years
     4.-BOEING, Administrator, EDP Manufacturing, 2 Years
     5.-SEATTLE FIRST BANK, Administrator Development and
Purchasing, 2 Years
     6.-U.S. NAVY, EDP Administration, 5 Years

EXPERIENCE
* IBM compatible PC's and Apples (as user)
* IBM compatible PC's and Apples (as technician)
* Databases, spreadsheets and word processing with msworks
and word perfect for PC's
    and main frames
* Netware 3.12
* Lan / Wan experienced (user)
* Hardware installation, assembly, testing, configurations
and troubleshooting
* Negotiated computer software and hardware changes with
vendors
* System documentation of software and hardware and user
instructions
* Prepared user menus and batch files for programs
* Team Leader for changes and implementation of changes
* Preparation of area procedures and job descriptions
* Preparation of some types of management reports
* Negotiated cost reduction efforts and implementations for
EDP and manual systems
* Preparation of some types of cost estimates and ROI
calculations

EDUCATION

BA degree - UNIVERSITY OF OKLAHOMA
MBA degree - NATIONAL UNIVERSITY
Continuing Training with Santa Fe Technical College in
computers and networking

CHRONOLOGICAL RESUME

Gene Merhish
984 La Paz Rd.

Placentia, CA   92670

(714) 996-4221

_____

2/93 to Present   ELECTRO CHEMICAL ETCH METAL
MARKINGS, INC., Brea, CA
              Sales and Marketing Manager

Recruited, trained and motivated national and international
sales force. Developed, upgraded and executed national
advertising programs and incentives. Expanded business on
an international level. Developed sales and marketing plan.
Developed new markets, customers and leads for sales force.
Improved customer capture rate and enhanced overall
performance and efficiency. Sold metal working systems.

7/91 to 11/93   PROTECH SYSTEMS, Chino, CA
              National Sales and Marketing Manager

Supervised 80 to 100 independent reps selling machine tool
guarding equipment. Recruited, trained and motivated
national sales force. Developed, upgraded and executed
national advertising programs and incentives. Expanded
business on an international level to several countries.
Organized, managed and conducted industrial shows and safety
seminars. Developed sales and marketing plan. Developed
new markets, customers and leads for sales force.

5/90 to 4/91   TRU-FORM INDUSTRIES, Santa Fe Springs,
CA
              National Sales Manager

Manager overseeing 30 to 40 independent reps selling
stampings, springs and wire forms. Recruited, trained and
motivated sales force. Improved customer capture rate and
pricing on metal products. Enhanced overall performance and
efficiency.

Gene Merhish
984 La Paz Rd.

Placentia, CA   92670

(714) 996-4221

_____

12/85 to 3/90   ACCURATE AIR ENGINEERING, Compton, CA
                       Systems Consultant

Planned, developed, quoted, designed, and sold compressed
air systems and components; including compressors, dryers,
after coolers, and filtration. Consultant for
manufacturing/processing company selling compressed air
components. Developed successful marketing program.
Created promotional video for sales department, improving
customer awareness. Designed and created training manual.
Generated new product lines expanding customer base.
Improved sales and marketing plan of the company's products
and services. I designed and created training manual to
improve understanding of responsibilities and duties. I
generated new product lines expanding customer base for the
firm. I was involved in improving sales and marketing plan.
While employed with the firm I was honored as Top Sales
Representative. I was responsible for assisting sales reps
in closing sales.

1982 to 12/85   FEMCO, North Salt Lake, UT
                       President & General Manager

I managed small-size company selling special production
equipment and related products. I introduced a special
state-of-the art oil production system to market place. I
presented new products to the industry. Identified target
markets for the company broadening customer base. I
arranged special purchases and advanced payments. I
negotiated sales to large national oil company. I planned
and executed all sales activity for the region. Composed
marketing letters and brochures with limited budget. I
trained and motivated distributors. I also established new
markets in western states enlarging customer base for the
firm. Reduced expenses and increased exposure of company
products.

Gene Merhish
984 La Paz Rd.

Placentia, CA   92670

(714) 996-4221

_____

1980 to 1982   UNICO, Salt Lake, UT
                General Plant & Marketing Manager

I managed and marketed large rotary equipment repair
company. I supervised 14 people while in this position. I
improved staffing of repair and service department. I
increased sales to $550,000 per month. I reduced operating
cost, increased gross profits to 75%, and lowered overhead.
I improved customer relations by problem solving. I worked
with mining processing companies in the Intermountain West
region. I developed, executed sales and marketing plan. I
oversaw direct mail and tele-marketing programs for the
company to improve overall business. I maintained high
profit margin during my employ. Trained and Supervised
sales force.

1977 to 1980   FOLSOM ASSOCIATES, Salt Lake, UT
                Sales Manager

As a manager I oversaw 5 direct salespersons for compressed
air equipment business. I was involved in building a solid
sales and marketing team. I was able to produce better team
work and market penetration. With my direction we captured
the largest single screw compressor from competition. I
increased sales to over $1 million per year that was over a
20% increase over the previous year. I worked with all
major processing and manufacturing companies in the
Intermountain West region. I developed sales and marketing
plan. I trained Industrial Sales Representative and
assisted in closing sales.

EDUCATION

    Masters Degree in Business/Secondary Administration,
Marketing, Sales
        Completed at California State University, San Jose, CA

154

Bachelors Degree in Business, Business Education
Completed at California State University, San Jose, CA

Associates Arts Degree in Business Administration
Completed at Western Wyoming Junior College, Rocks
Springs, Wyo.

CHRONOLOGICAL RESUME

Gene
Merhish
984 La Paz Rd.

Placentia, CA 92670

(714) 996-4221

_____

Present   COLE INSTRUMENTS, Santa Ana, CA
                 Regional Sales Manager

Recruit, train and motivate a national sales force. Develop
and execute national advertising programs and incentives.
Expansion of business nationally and in Canada. Generate
new sales. Develop new markets, customers and leads for the
sales force. Improve customer capture rate and enhance
overall performance and efficiency. Assist in resolving
customer complaints, quoting product prices and
participating in presales discussions with customers. The
focus of sales is in rotary switches.

7/91 to 11/93   PROTECH SYSTEMS, Chino, CA
                 National Sales and Marketing Manager

Supervised 80 to 100 independent reps selling machine tool
guarding equipment. Recruited, trained and motivated
national sales force. Developed, upgraded and executed
national advertising programs and incentives. Expanded
business on an international level to several countries.
Organized, managed and conducted industrial shows and safety
seminars. Developed sales and marketing plan. Developed
new markets, customers and leads for sales force.

5/90 to 4/91   TRU-FORM INDUSTRIES, Santa Fe Springs,
CA
                 National Sales Manager

Manager overseeing 30 to 40 independent reps selling
stampings, springs and wire forms. Recruited, trained and
motivated sales force. Improved customer capture rate and
pricing on metal products. Enhanced overall performance and
efficiency.

Gene Merhish
984 La Paz Road
Placentia, CA 92670

714-996-4221

12/85 to 3/90   ACCURATE AIR ENGINEERING, Compton, CA
                                 Systems Consultant

Planned, developed, quoted, designed, and sold compressed air systems and components; including compressors, dryers, aftercoolers, and filtration. Consultant for manufacturing/processing company selling compressed air components. Developed successful marketing program. Created promotional video for sales department, improving customer awareness. Designed and created training manual. Improved sales and marketing plan.

1982 to 12/85   FEMCO, N. Salt Lake, UT
                                 President/General Manager

Managed small-size company selling special oil field down-hole production equipment and related products. Introduced a special state-of-the-art oil production system to market place. Presented new products to the industry. Identified target markets for the company broadening customer base. Arranged special purchases And advanced payments. Negotiated sales to large national oil companies. Planned and executed all sales activities for the region. Composed marketing letters and brochures with limited budget. Trained and motivated distributors. Established new markets in western states enlarging customer base. Reduced expenses and increased exposure of company products.

1980 to 1982   UNICO, Salt Lake, UT
                                 General Plant & Marketing Manager

Managed and marketed large rotary equipment repair company. Supervised 16 people. Improved staffing of repair and service department. Increased sale to over $250,000 per month. Reduced operation cost by 12 percent, and lowered overhead by 8.5 percent. Improved customer relations by resolving problems. Worked with mining, processing, oil production, and refinery in the Intermountain West region.

1977 to 1980   FOLSOM ASSOCIATES, Salt Lake, UT
                                 Sales Manager

Manager of Compressed Air Division. Overseen 5 direct salespersons for compressed air equipment business. Also managed Service Department. Built a solid sales and marketing team. Improved team work and increased market penetration. Captured the largest single screw compressor sale in the history of compressed air sales in Utah for the company and from the competition. Increased sales to over one million dollars per year. Worked with major processing, manufacturing, and mining companies in the Intermountain West region.

EDUCATION

   Masters Degree in Business/Secondary Administration, Marketing and Sales
   Completed at California State University, San Jose, CA

   Bachelors Degree in Business, Business Education/Business Administration
   Completed at California State University, San Jose, CA

CHRONOLOGICAL RESUME

Gene Merhish   984 La Paz Road, Placentia, CA 92870
714-996-4221

Objective seeking a leadership role opportunity where I can use my many years of experience, education, and training in assisting a progressive company in building a profitable business as we transition into the 21st century. As an be it in teaching or administration.

- Supervision   Advertising   Training
- Closing The Sale   Design Engineering   Increase Profit
- Managed Industrial Shows seminars   Developed marketing plans
- Target Marketing   Team player   Forecasting
- Supervision Turn-key Installation   Pricing Enthusiastic
- Media and Advertising Selection   Negotiation   Computer Knowledge
- P & L   Closing the Sales   Trouble Shooting
- Guidance   Motivation   Instruction
- Understanding   Caring   Empirical

9/97 to Presently   **CENTINELA VALLEY UNION HIGH SCHOOL DISTRICT**
                       Full-Time Teacher, Swift Program

Currently teaching in an alternation program that is an opportunity class for students who have behavior and attendance problems. Developed curriculum, classroom logistics, and other support systems. Also have improved and enhanced student learning by obtaining community support to donate nearly $400,000 worth of computer systems and other related items. Have been involved in conflict resolution and classroom management techniques that have reduced home and in-house suspensions. Improving attendance. By 30 percent.

On my own time, I have been training to gain experience in administrative activities. Also have worked with students to make sure they follow rules and regulations of the school. I am fully credentialed as a business teacher, vocational education teacher, at both the High School and Adults levels, plus junior college and university. I also hold an administrative credential. See enclosed experience sheet for additional work experience in Education.

5/98 to Presently   **IVY UNIVERSITY, Alhambra, CA**
                       Instructor Graduate and Undergraduate Classes

As an Instructor at Ivy University, I teach Marketing and Management courses. I work with mostly Chinese students. Most of these students are full-time in Undergraduate or Graduate programs in Business, Marketing, Computers, or Administrative courses here at the University.

Gene Merhish   984 La Paz Road, Placentia, CA 92870
714-996-4221

9/95 to 9/97   ORANGE COUNTY DEPT. OF EDUCATION, Costa Mesa, CA
                       Long-term Sub. Teacher

As a teacher in Alternative and Correctional Education, I taught and offered counseling to lthe students within said programs. I have offered instructional guidance. I have taught in a number of programs that Orange County has to offer, such as the Horizon program, YGC (Trreatment Facility Housing), Alternative Education, AP classes, and more. I offered a positive role model, current and advanced teaching techniques. These students represented a variance of students that have committed a variety of felony crimes ans well as students at risk. My work for the County has been at all grade levels.

1/96 to 12/31/96   OSO HOME CARE, Irvine, CA
                       Marketing & Sales Manager

Developed and executed regional marketing plan, advertising programs, news releases, Newsletter, tele-marketing, and direct mail programs. Expansion of business by generating new sales and customers (patients) for the company was one of my successes. Developed current and new markets, customers, and leads. Improved customer, patients capture rate that enhanced overall performance and efficiency was achieved from my efforts. Assisted in resolving customer complaints, developed and negotiated contracts with major regional and national accounts. Participating in pre-sales discussions, presentations, and inservice with major Medical Groups, HMOs, IPAs, and PPOs were a few of my functions. The focus of sales was in Infusion Therapy, Surgical Supplies, DME, and related services. I worked closely with the President of the company to develop more contracts in the history of the company. Because of major internal problems within the organization, all marketing and advertising activities were discontinued to concentrate on collections and operation of the Pharmacy. With this choice I was seeking a new challenge.

7/91 to 11/93   PROTECH SYSTEMS, Chino, CA
                       National Sales & Marketing Manager

I supervised 80 to 100 independent reps selling machine tool guarding equipment. Recruited, trained, and motivated national sales force. I developed, upgraded, and executed national advertising program via news releases, direct mailing, composed marketing letters, and advertising. I expanded business on an international level to several countries. I organized, managed and conducted industrial shows and safety seminars. I developed sales and marketing plan. Developed new markets, customers and leads for sales force. I developed new markets, customers and leads for sales one of my responsibilities was to assist sales reps in closing sales. After two major "downsizings" of the company, management decided to discontinue all marketing activities and terminating my position and ride out the recession.

5/90 to 4/91   TRU-FORM INDUSTRIES, Santa Fe Springs, CA
                       National Sales & Marketing Manager

Manager overseeing 30 to 40 independent reps selling stampings, springs, and wire forms. Recruited, trained and motivated sales force. Improved customer capture rate and pricing on metal products. Developed news releases, composed marketing letters, advertising, and direct mail programs. Conducted industrial shows. Enhanced overall performance and efficiency. Acquired experience with injection molding. Developed quotes, product pricing, and assisted sales reps in closing sales.

12/85 to 3/90   ACCURATE AIR ENGINEERING, Compton, CA
                                            Systems Consultant and Engineer

I Planned, developed, quoted, designed, and sold compressed air systems and components including compressors, dryers, aftercoolers, and filtration. I was Cosultant for manufacturing and procession company selling compressed air components. I developed a successful marketing program and executed it. I created promotional video for sales department, improving customer awareness and selling company capabilities. I designed and created training manual for training new sales people. I generated new product lines expanded customer base. I improved sales and the company's business. I was honored as Top Sales Representative. I success in the selling of Compressed Air Systems and related management responsibility within or outside the Compressed Air Industry. My major intent was to find a growth industry where I could fully use my marketing and management.

1982 to 12/85   FEMCO, North Salt Lake, Utah
                                            President and General Manager

Managed small company selling special oil field down-hole production equipment and related products. Introduced a special state-of-art oil production system to market place. Negotiated large national oil company sales. Trained and motivated distributors. Established new markets and increase exposure of company products.

Gene Merhish   984 La Paz Road, Placentia, CA 92670
714-996-4221

COLE INSTRUMENT, Santa Ana, CA
Regional Sales Manager

Recruited, trained and motivated a National sales force. Developed and executed National advertising programs. And incentives. Expansion of the business nationally and in Canada. Generating new sales, developing new markets, customers, and leads for the sales force were part of my responsibility. Also improved customer capture rate and the enhancement of the overall performance and efficiency of the territory were my tasks. Furthermore, I was involved in resolving customer complaints. Was responsible for quotations, pricing, and contract negotiation. Participated in pre-sale discussions, Engineering, with customers. The focus of the company was the sale of "high tech" rotary switches. I was "downsized" because of a failing economy.

GARDNER DENVER, South San Francisco, CA
Regional Manager

This position was concerned with the development of new customers and the expansion of relationships with existing customers. The job consisted field application, engineering, and consultation on the air application of compressors and related equipment. The ultimate goal was to promote produce, service, maximize sales volume. Duties included the motivation and training of Distributive Salesman and the supervised the operation of the service department and coordinated sales with sales force. Also involved in working with Engineering to design in equipment. Left firm to relocate to another state.

HAYWARD UNIFIED SCHOOL DISTRICT, ROC/P
Instructor, Vocational Education (Retailing)

In this position I was involved in the training of 10th through 12th grade students in the fundamentals of Retail Merchandising. We operated a community based retailing store with an associated classroom. The students were training in all areas of Cashiering, Sales, Management, Pricing, and more. The program drew students from five (5) high schools in the Hayward area. This program was one of the most advanced programs of its kind in the Western States. It became a demonstration program for the State of California. In addition, I was selected to consultant for the Department of program DECA program and many of them placed in State competition in various categories.

HARNISCHFEGER, San Francisco, CA
Regional Manager

As the Regional Manager I was responsible for the sales of a full line of welding equipment and systems. I assisted my distributors in the sales of said equipment and welding problems. Assisted in establishing relationships between new major customers and the distributors. Increased sales over previous year by 20 percent. Company was sold and the position was eliminated.

LOCKHEED MISSILE & SPACE CO., Sunnyvale, CA
System Technical

I was involved in systems checkout (pneumatic, hydraulic) on the Agena and Polaris guidance systems. Also Fabricated, mocked-up, assembled, tested equipment and systems for flight. I was also involved in research and development of applications of plastics and resins for encapsulation of electronic components.

Education

Masters Degree in Secondary Administration/Marketing
Completed at California State University, San Jose, CA

Bachelors Degree in Business, Business Education
Completed at California State University, San Jose, CA

Marital Status

Married, four Adult children

Height & Weigh

6'3", 225 pounds, range

Military Service

United States Navy, Army & Air Force Reserves, and National Guard

CHRONOLOGICAL RESUME

Bill Gates
Post Office Box 123
Denver, Co 92341
303-983-7622 (Home)
303-983-5321 (Office)

BACKGROUND SUMMARY

Fifteen years experience in mining industry with eight years
in a supervisory position. Skilled in driving main entries,
long wall entries, and pillar work. Capable of operating
all underground machinery. Planned cutting sequence, power
center, and belt moves. Established high production record
and exemplary safety history.

WORK EXPERIENCE

SUPERIOR COAL, Golden, Colorado   July 1974
to Present
Section Foreman - July 1984 to 1986
Construction Foreman - July 1974 to July 1984
Responsible for a nine man production crew. Produced coal
in safe manner on conventional and continuous miner shifts.
Maintained ventilation and coordinated with maintenance.

DUNLOP SAND AND GRAVEL, INC., Denver, Colorado   May 1992
to June 1994

Mechanic and Truck Driver
Responsibilities included fueling diesel engine on gravel
crusher, making belt repairs, doing mechanic work when
crusher broke down, building rolls with automatic welder,
and driving five yard dump truck.

EDUCATION
Western Wyoming Junior, Rock Springs, Wyo., A.A.S. -
Political Science, 1972.
Rock Springs High School, Rock Springs, Wyo., 1970

FUNCTIONAL RESUME

Bobbie Jo
Jingle
456 West Iowa Street
Los Angeles, CA 90022
310-995-2222 Home
310-885-5667 Work

BACKGROUND SUMMARY

Eighteen years of progressively responsible nursing
experience in hospital, public health, and with mental
health agencies.

STAFF NURSING Experience in Level I & II nurseries. Main
emphasis included UA   lines and chest tubes.
Maintained RDS infants requiring less than   50%
oxygen. Maintained criteria for quality patient care.
                    Performed staff evaluations and service
ratings.

PUBLIC HEALTH Coordinated scheduling and procedures in
clinics for patients with   orthopedic
handicaps, cerebral palsy, and learning disabilities.
                    Established immunization program. Served as
school nurse to six   area schools. Promoted
individual, family, and community health   by
direct nursing care and teaching/supervision of patients.
                    Supervised LPNs and Aides in patients'
homes.

TRAINING   Handled assessment of staff needs for inservice education.   Designed,
implemented and/or conducted programs for staff
    development. Assisted in same for hospital-wide
programs.   Conducted unit-based orientation
for new staff

SUPERVISION   Established criteria and standards of nursing
care for approximately   125 acutely disturbed
hospitalized patients. Supervised 2 shift
    supervisors, 5 head nurses, and approximately 125 R.N.s
and   attendants. I was also involved in the
interviewing and hiring of   new employees. I
evaluated staff performance. Assisted in budget

planning, policies, and procedures. In addition to the above, I acted   as a consultant to other hospital departments.

Bobbie Jo Jingle
Page 2.

EXPERIENCE

LAKEVIEW HOSPITAL	Lakeview, CA	1981-1984
PLACENTIA GENERAL HOSPITAL	Placentia, CA	1976-1981
GARDEN GROVE HOSPITAL	Garden Grove, CA	1973-1975
BREA GENERAL HOSPITAL	Brea, CA	1970-1973
PUBLIC HEALTH OF CALIFORNIA	Santa Ana, CA	1968-1970

EDUCATION

B.S. Nursing, University Los Angeles, Los Angeles, CA - May 1968

Continuing Education:

"Care of the High Risk Neonate" - June 1985
"Preceptor Development Program" - May 1983
"Breast feeding the Premature Infant" - November 1975
"Advanced Concepts of Neonatal Nursing" - December 1974
"National Conference of Neonatal Nursing" - October 1974

PROFESSIONAL ORGANIZATIONS

American Nurses Association
California Nurses Association
National Association of Neonatal Nurses

COMBINATION RESUME

Debi E. Dodds
45 Main Street
Littletown, New Jersey   48221
201-333-6565

CAREER SUMMARY

MBA with over eleven (11) years of diversified and
progressive marketing experience. Skilled in all aspects of
product development, commercialization, and management of
new products.

Experienced in development of new markets and acquisitions
of food processing chemicals, weighing and measurement
instruments, inorganic industrial chemicals, and
architectural coil products.

PROFESSIONAL EXPERIENCE

Shell Oil Corporation
August 1979 to Present
Oiltown, New Jersey

Commercial Development Analyst   (1982 to Present)

Commercial Development Specialist   (1979 to 1982)

Managed new product development from identification through
development, market introduction, and commercialization.
Managed diversification program in food processing chemicals
area.

    Researched and recommended market entry with
acquisition of four organizations,   each with sales 15 -
25 million.

    Managed development and commercialization of
architectural coil product with   sales potential of 6
million.

    Managed development of three chrome-free treatments
with combined sales   potential of 25 million.

DEBI E. DODDS
Page Two

Lowland Chemical Corporation
February 1978 to now
Midway, New Jersey

Market Research Associate

Researched and identified new products as well as determined
required product characteristics and cost constraints.
Directed and managed field trials for new products.

　　　Recommended organization changes which reduced payroll
expenses by seven　　percent.

　　　Identified need for and directed market study of new
design for surgical blade　　which verified market
acceptability.

　　　Investigated required features and performance of
arterial monitoring system which　resulted in its
successful marketing introduction.

KTM Industries, Inc.
June 1976 to February 1978
Jamestown, New Jersey

Market Research Analyst

Responsibilities included sales forecasting and analysis.
Designed and handled mail and telephone surveys.

　　　Designed and directed study of new marketing vehicle
intended to sell more　　effectively specific market
segment.

EDUCATION

J.D. - Pacific Coast University, Long Beach, CA 1985.

M.B.A. - Marketing - San Jose State University, San Jose, CA
1976.

B.A. - English - University of Nevada, 1974.

Implemented new product review procedure which synthesized opinions of all   concerned departments into focused R & D work.

Implemented training program for sales and technical services which reduced   product handling problems in market introduction phase.

THE TAILOR-MADE RESUME

Cory (CJ) Dodds
123 Casino Street
Las Vegas, NV 27514

EXPERIENCE:
November 1983
to Present: Current employer is a top financial
institution.

March 1985
to Present: Assistant Vice President -
Commercial Lending

          Handling a $15 million portfolio consisting
of approximately 210   accounts. Portfolio
consisting of : Accounts Receivable, Real
     Estate, Airplane, Inventory, and Equipment Lending.
Dealing with   credit of $10,000 to $5 million.

1983 to 1985   Credit Analyst - Loan Review

          Credit Analysis, Documentation Review, Loan
Department Reports,   Review of Documentation
in Credit Files, Credit Quality.

1978 - 1983   Assistant Bank Examiner Nevada Bank
Regulatory   Commission

          Examination of banks, conducted appraisal and
review of loans.   Audited internal controls and
records. Review of compliance and   consumer
regulations

EDUCATION: Jurist Doctor in Law
                    Pacific Coast University
                 Masters Degree in Business
Administration - Finance
                    University of Nevada
                 Bachelor of Science Degree - Psychology
                    Cal State Fullerton, CA

CONTINUING
EDUCATION: Bank Auditing & Accounting School
                 Trust Examination School

Compliance School (Consumer Regulations)
Loan Review & Analysis School

REFERENCES: Available Upon Request.

Chapter Nineteen

Stationery

You should always use the best stationary that you can afford. All correspondence to any organization may result in either you getting the job or losing it. It can go either way. You never know.

You may be judged solely on your stationary. You should always type any responses to any questions on good stationary. They may tell you just write a quick note. There is no such thing as just a quick note when you applying for job.

Anything you submit may be put in your file and stay there for a long time. Anytime anyone sees that File may judge you based on whatever they see. This may or may not be your best work. Always be careful about who will see it later and what reactions they may have.

Remember to use the best to impress!

Chapter Twenty

How Should I Dress?

The first few seconds may be all you get to make that lasting impression. This may be surprising to you, nevertheless, it is true. Think about when you see or meet a man or woman. We all make judgments. In the first few seconds when we meet them. The impression we get may or may not be fair, but the judgment is made. We may adjust or change our opin- ion over time, and then again we may not. Dress for your success! People rarely change their opinion of you at an interview once it is set. They will not want to admit to an error.

We have interviewed thousands of people for various jobs in various compa- nies. The first few minutes of any interview will decide if you are going to get the job or not. The interview may last hours longer, but the final decision is cut and dry in the first few minutes.

The key question is why. The reason appears to be that if the interviewer likes you, you will get the job. You will shown the door if the interviewer does not like you.

Your clothes may help you get the job.

A man should wear conservation clothes to an interview. A woman should do the same. Do nothing outlandish or fancy. You should be conservative in all respects.

We do not want to over or under dress. This is true of anyone. You should always be in good taste. Men can wear a "power suit". We like a three piece black suit black suit with a coordinating shirt, tie and black shoes. Women should generally wear a dark dress with little or no make up. Avoid over-sized, way out earnings, nose rings, or any way out accessories. Wearing too much make up may detract from you and the interview. Try to wear something which you would like to see if you were doing the interviewing.
Let's talk for a moment about smoking. You may or may not smoke. Fewer and fewer people smoke today. Many offices and companies are non-smoking. There appears to little to stop the no smoking movement. You should not smoke during an interview. This is true even if you see a smoking permitted sign.

Hair

The smoke permeates your clothes, hair and the like. You will sink to the non-smoker. So here is a word to the wise: if you have to smoke, do it in other clothing and before you clean up to go to the interview. Shower before the interview.

Let us talk about hair. We like long hair to a point and so will the interviewer. We have been told a story about one salesperson who had grown his hair very long. The longer his hair got, the less business he did. Now we do not know if this is a true story or not, or if it has happened to you, but unless you are interviewing tor a "Rock Band," keep the length in good taste.

For men , keep your hair trimmed neatly but not shaved. Women should have neat hair for all interviews. Long hair to the floor may be great for the " Believe it or not" book but it has no place at an interview.

Avoid gum, candy, and anything you could be eating during the interview. Any of this kind of stuff can get points taken away from your interviewing performance.

Just a word on drinks at the interview. Try to get your coffee or drinks before or after the interview. Do not accept a drink of coffee (even if one is offered) at the interview. There are only three things that can happen with drinks at the interview and all are bad. Tell the interviewer thanls but you just had a drink.

Always shine your shoes before the interview. Some interviews are lost on bad shoes alone. Wash you're your hands and keep your finger nails cleaned and well cut.

Note

During your research, find out how the interviewer dresses and how much emphasis the company puts on "proper business attire". If you can , see these people before the interview in person nad see how they are dressed. Follow the company rules if you know them.

Chapter Twenty-one

The Pre-Interview

There are several things that you can do to assist you in being successful. The employer wants a well-rounded person who will be successful in business and in their personal and community life. They are particularly eager to employ those who can produce in their business as quickly as possible. The employer inquires about attitudes, past performance, and background when some applies for a job. The employers base their decision on many things including:

1. Interest in the business.
2. A strong desire to work and learn the business.
3. Be able to speak good and clear English.
4. Previous work experience.
5. Specific educational preparation.
6. Use of leisure time and community participation.
7. Good health and personal habits.
8. Personal appearance and manners.
9. Special skills and abilities.
10. Etc.

Some of these factors may be more important than others but all are considered at least in passing.

The Telephone

The telephone is your best friend. You should always use it accordingly. The phone is one of the most important tools you have for your job search. You should know how to use it and use it well. The telephone can be the difference between you getting the job and not getting it. Always use the methods discussed here when you are calling an employer.

Practice each point in this book before you attempt to call an employer. You should not leave anything to chance. Practice your call before you make it. Go over what you are going to say and do it with someone else.

How to use the phone

- Put a smile on your face before you pick up the phone. The phone lines will carry your smile, as well as a scowl, depression, or hostility. Your smile will carry over the phone as you grin from ear to ear.
- When you are talking on the phone, do it front of a a mirror near your phone. mirror. You should have
- It is easier to say "NO" to a person who just sounds negative over the phone. You need to practice with an unbiased or friendly before making a call. It is impossible at say "NO" to a positive, friendly per- son.

Construct a phone approach using the information you have gathered about the job you have gathered about the job you are interested in applying for

Use three (3) short paragraphs to build an interesting, attention-getting conversation.

A– First, you opening statement must be a "grabber." You have got to get the attention of the listener. On the lines below, write a statement that gets the attention of the person you are calling:

_____
_____
_____
_____

B- Next, you phone call needs to generate and build "desire." Write a statement herein that will generate desire.

_____
_____
_____
_____

C- In the last statement, you need to bring the listener to "action." Write a statement below that calls for action on the part of the listener.

_____
_____
_____
_____

Since you know that the firm is looking for someone to fill the position in question, do not allow the listener to hang up before you determine you can come in for an interview.

Always use the same script when you are calling an employer. Know what you want to say before you say it. Be ready with answers for any objections as to why they cannot see you for an interview. Always ask if Monday or Tuesday would be better for the interview. This eliminates the possibility of rejection.

Try to improve your script after every call. Write down "key" points and questions and review your answers. Again if possible, review them with a friend.

Questions To Ask At The Initial Contact From A Prospective Employer

Keep This Information Handy By Your Phone For Interview Information

- Ask the name of person to whom you are speaking....his or her title? Ask for the spelling if unusual....or just to be safe.

- What is the exact name of the company? Telephone number.

- Where will this meeting be held? Cross streets? Landmarks? Building #?

- What is the name and title of the person with whom you will be meeting....exact spelling if unusual.

    * Title of the position you will be discussing.
    * What is the company's product or service?
    * What is their size? Sales? Number of employees?
    * Is sit a division, branch or subsidiary or another company?
    * Is the company privately held or a publicly traded corporation?
    * What is the name of the parent— or—corporate company?
    * Where is the company headquartered?
    * Please forward to me a copy of your financial report.

>**Be Certain To Call And Reschedule If Something Prevents You From Being Right on Time.**

>**Give Yourself Plenty Of Time For Unforeseen Difficulties Such As Parking, Traffic, Etc.**

_____

_____

_____

_____

Chapter Twenty-Two

The Interview

The interview is the key to getting a job. You cannot rest until you have that key in your pocket. There may be a conflict between your ideas and the goals of future employer. You should always be evaluating the situation for any possibility of conflict. You may have to examine your options many times, and above all, you must remain flexible. You should try to resolve any conflicts if you can, But you should be ready to take another job if you cannot. There are gray areas you should carefully examine before your interview.

You should have a ready answer for any questions on the "gray" areas in your background. Do not attempt to invent an answer during the interview. This will almost always go badly.

You should have   already thought about what your are going to say. Gray areas
could be periods   of unemployment or when you were underemployed, out of the
country, or when   you were in jail. They could be bad companies who will not
enhance your re-   sume or give you a good recommendation, but
You have worked   for them. We have worked for firms that wouldn't look good on
our resumes, but   they did provide a means to an end by providing short-term employment and some you must do what you can to get by.

Be aware that the employer/interviewer already has an image in his/her mind of what he/she wants for this job. Your job is to fit his/her image to a tee. The first impression is the most important thing. The first minute usually determines if you get the job. You should make it your best!!!

Your selling task is to attract his/her favorable attention. You do this by being well-groomed, ready, poised and friendly. You know you have succeeded when he/she returns the your smile.

Answer the interviewer's questions directly and truthfully. Use correct English and avoid slang. Do not interrupt the interviewer. Be prepared to answer questions about why you want to work for this organization, your hobbies, interests, part-time work experience and long-   term goals. Remember to stress your qualifications for the job. Your responsibilities is   this meeting include selling yourself and your goals. Be definite!! Be interesting and   interested! Try to fit into what they are looking for. Show them you can do this job.

The interviewer will give you a chance to ask questions in   most cases. This is your opportunity to learn more about the nature and requirements for   this job. You may want to formulate some questions in advance to ask the interviewer.   You then have the right to ask even more questions about the job. If you are offered this   job, don't ask about salary, benefits, vacation policy, etc. Immediately. The interviewer may not offer you the job if he thinks this is all you are interested in.

The interviewer attempt to trap you. Be careful what you say. You may be nervous during the interview. Try to relax, be calm. Take a few deep breaths. You should be as honest as possible, but try to remember any comments you say that are negative may result in your not getting the position. Be positive at all times. Remember that the interview may continue until after you walk out the door and to your car. (Be on guard).

You may lose a job on the way to your car by saying something "stupid," by being asked a question out-of-the-blue and you not being prepared with the right answer. Also, avoid giving opinions about individuals or other executives. You never know where loyalties lie on the part of the interviewer.

You should "dry-run" interviews and your cover letter and resume with a friend or family member before you go to the real thing. Your spouse can be helpful in this area. In addition, you can get valuable feedback from your friend or spouse if you discuss what occurred in the interview. This is like a military "debriefing." Like the military debriefing, the material from the interview is fresh in your mind and you may not omit "key" details of what was said in the interview.

Try to write everything you said in detail on a piece of paper in order to review what happened for future interviews. Always try to improve on what you say.

You should be comfortable with your resume and your cover letter. One student included on his resume that he was a member of the school Glee Club. During the interview, the interviewer saw this and mentioned that he was a member of the same Glee Club 20 years ago. They then spent two (2) hours talking about the Glee Club. It goes with saying that the student got the job. If the applicant had never mentioned the club, the job would have possibly gone elsewhere.

You will never know what will pop up in a interview. You should be prepared for anything. Try to put yourself in the best light! Put yourself in the interviewer's place. What is the interviewed interested in?

Your resume should always be written to show the future employer that you are there to help them solve their problems. You should follow up on this during the interview.

You are not there so you can get great pay and benefits. Your resume should be written with your experience as it relates to the job they want to fill. Show them you have the same type of work experience and transferable skills. You must convince them you are the greatest person ever for this job . Sell yourself!

The first few minutes an interviewee spends with an interviewer are probably the most important in the entire presentation. This cannot be said too many times! Unless you, the interviewee, can get the favorable attention of interviewer at the start of the interview, it is very hard to gain lost ground later.

A good beginning is important. The approach to use requires preparation and attention to detail on your part. The specialty, wholesale, or industrial interviewee should make a thorough study of the interviewer's company before the meeting, making sure to cover everything including the specific characteristics of personality traits. This information may be hard to come by, but it should be obtained if possible. Sometimes it is possible to talk to customers, suppliers, or even the competition to gain insight and information.

As an interviewee, you have an excellent opportunity to gain some knowledge of the company and to develop a relationship with the interviewer. Also, by reviewing what is in th office, you can get some idea of what the interviewer is interested in. There may be pictures or objects that the interviewer is interested in displayed.

No matter how well the interviewee has prepared his or her presentation for the interview or how well he/she knows the

Possible questions, he/she cannot expect to conduct a successful interview unless he/she can gain a favorable impression. You must get the interviewer on your side. The interviewer must that you are a good candidate to spend time with.

Avoid name-dropping or phony compliments these are excellent way to blow and interview. Remember be sincere and sell yourself with humility. If the interviewer mentions he is proud of his 68 golfing score, you may have a great anxiety growing inside of you to tell him you shot a 67— but fight the tendency. Say nothing, and simply respond, "That's very good!" If he asks if you golf and what your best score is, you of course, can say so, but add, "I think that I played at a must easier course, as I ordinarily am not that good."

Evaluating If You Have Sold Yourself Well?

1. When the interviewer says, "You remind me of my self."
2. When he/she calls other members of the company to step into the office to meet you.
3. When he/she starts selling you on their organization or business as hard as you sold yourself.
4. When the interviewer shows her/she is comfortable talking to you.
5. When he/she gives you a tour of the plant, or business, introducing you to people as you progress.
6. When the interview lasts more than thirty minutes.
7. When he/she asks, "When would you ba available to start work?'
8. When he/she goes into great detail explaining the fringe benefits of the organization.
9. When he/she asks, "What kind of a starting salary are you looking for/"
10. When he/she starts talking about positions you can advance to after you have been with the firm for awhile.

Questions You May Want To Ask Once You Are Sure They Are Interested In You

First, you might preface your questioning by stating, "Before I throw my heart and soul into this position, I'd like to make sure this is the right job for me, so if it's OK with you, I'd like to ask you a few questions."

May we point out that by asking sound, intelligent, well thought out questions, you will enhance the probability of your getting the position. A candidate who has no questions to ask conveys the idea that thinking is not one of his/her strong suits.

1. Is this a new position?
2. Has there been high turnover in this job.
3. Is the person who had this position last still with the company? If so, would it be possible for me to talk to him/her?
4. Are openings for the better positions in this firm generally filled from within?
5. If I do an exemplary job, when might I expect to be promoted?
6. Are there problems with this position which need solving?
7. Is there a written job description for this position that I might take a look at? (Ask this question only if you have not obtained one.)

8. What is the average work week of the individual filling this position?
9. What does the future of this firm look like to you?
10. Do you feel that most of the employees who work here enjoy coming in everyday?
11. Is there any chance I will be asked to relocate or travel?
12. Will I be responsible to answer to just one person, or will I have a multitude of bosses?
13. Are there any serious problems the company is experiencing now?
14. Is there any probability the company will be sold?
15. Do you have any questions or concerns about my ability to do this job?
16. When do you expect to make a hiring decision relevant to this position?

If you have other questions you want to ask the interviewer—write them here

_____
_____
_____
_____
_____
_____
_____
_____
_____
_____
_____
_____
_____
_____
_____
_____
_____
_____
_____

Closing the interview

Closing the interview is like closing a sale, all good salesperson knows you must ask for the order. In this case, you must ask for the position or job.

A intelligent interviewer knows that a person who shows he really wants the position will most probably be a better candidate and employee. If you have concluded that "this is the position for me," then, by goodness go after it with conviction.

Here are a few examples:

A– Thank you for the interview, Mr. Lambert, I' am very impressed with both you and your firm. I'd like to go to work here, and believe me, if given a chance you will be proud of the job I do.

B- Mr. Ishibashi, I am excited at the prospect of working here. Just say the word and I am ready to start. I' m confident you will be pleased with my work!

Video Taping

Another idea whose time has come is video taping. This is one practice that we do in our classroom of Business and Careers classes. Most of us today have a camcorder or we have a friend who has one. You may want your friend to tape you more than once and ask you many of the basic interviewing questions we have been discussing. The questions are usually the same but may vary slightly.

One undergraduate student at a recent class was taped on the first day of class. The student thought he had done an excellent job and would have gotten the job if this was a real interview.

The class was asked to critique the interview after the tape was played back. The student discovered he did everything wrong. The video does not lie. The student wore a shirt with holes in it and was stained. The student was chewing gum. The student discovered that he was not dressed properly; he had no necktie or coat on. We think you get the idea. At the end of the course, the student was video taped again. He was perfectly ready for his "real" interview and a chance at that first job.

Recently, we were aware of another person who was interviewed for a bank job in an office with windows that turned into mirrors when the sun hit them. The applicant looked at himself in the "mirrored" windows during the entire interview. He never looked at the interviewer again during the 20 minute interview! We are sure you have figured out that the person never got the job and most likely did not even know what he did wrong.

Often a person can do things that may not be good in an interview and not even know it. You may be able to help your overall appearance and to correct any bad behaviors or mannerisms by using a video tape. The interviewer will judge you on your resume, application, references, cover letter, and appearance at the interview. They generally do not have anything else to go on. This is really very little information on which to base such an important decision. You have to cover all your bases before the final decision is reached. You must look as good as you can. Think about the fact that these impressions are made in the first few seconds of an interview, not minutes. And if you are going to try to go for a position, would it be worth a little time in from of a camcorder polishing your skills? We would suggest that you practice video interviewing as much as you can. Like any other skill, the more you do it, the better you become. Would you ever see a professional football player or tennis player not continue to polish their skills? After every football game, and certainly before the next game, the "pros" watch a video of how they played their last game and also the video of their competitors. You are a pro so watch and polish up for each game (interview) and the game of getting that job!

Body Language

There are many important components associated with getting a job; the resume, newsletter, and/or cover letter alone are not going to do it for you, unfortunately. These items working in concert hopefully get you in front of the interviewer. Now that you are in front of the person who holds "key" to your future of you going to work in their company or organization, you lmust use additional job seeking skills.

Note

Have pleasing facial expression?

Do you smile?

Good eye contact?

Appear friendly?

Appear friendly?

Walk with confidence?

Good gestures and mannerisms?

Are you annoying?

Yes, the message to send as you enter the room without saying a word selling you as the shine on your shoes or the crisp paper resume is printed on.

Often applicants will drift into the interviewer's office, plop down on a chair, begin to slouch, cross their legs, fold their hands behind their neck, and say, "ok, let's interview!

If you really want some-applicant, someone they organization. In many you to other members of tic about selling you is one to hire you, you must make them feel you are a worthy would be proud to have on their team or working in their cases, the interviewer is going to have to recommend or sell the company. The only way they are going to be enthusias-when you come across that way to them.

Your body language is another tool that can say qreat things about you or not. It can show poise, confidence, esteem, warmth, interest, sense of humor, and maturity. On the other hand, you body language can suggest disregard, immaturity, foolishness, disorder, gloom, apathy, stupidity, and so much more.

Every body movement tells a story so you need to practice in front of a mirror or in front of a video recorder until you body movements and gestures convey that appropriate message that is right for the job and projects the image of the organization you ant to work for. Remember, no gum and do not smoke; these two items will quickly get you shot down.

Talking To The Interviewer

Over 40 percent of your first impression will be from what you say and how you talk or what is heard. Therefore, your communication is still another component in getting the job. So we have to be careful of what we say and how we say it to be successful in our quest!

We know many of you will fight the suggestion of doing a mock interview, but it is your future. It is you who will benefit from this exercise. You have paid good money for this book. If it is going to do the job you ask of it, you must do your part.

Note

* How is your voice projection? Do you sound self-assured?

* How is your voice inflection? Do you talk in the monotone to much?

* How is your enunciation? Are you understood clearly?

* Do you talk too fast or too slowly?

* How is your expression? Do sound warm, friendly, interesting, enthusiastic?

* Do you sound knowledgeable? Do you sound scattered?

* Do you talk to much?

* Are you a good listener?

The last question, "are you a good listener?" needs to be discussed in more detail. As teachers over the years, we have talked to college students and high school students as the importance of listening. There are course on listening. But, like these students, many applicants may be outstanding in all other aspects of the interview, less one, they fail listening. The talk too much, not allowing the interviewer a chance to conduct the interview. These applicants believe that they have to spit out as much information as they can. It is hoped that, somehow, they finally learned to listen and that they are not still out there looking for a job and wondering why no one will hire them.

Be A Good Listener

If you know little to nothing about a subject, do not try to impress the interviewer with your stupidity! No matter if it is politics, hunting, car repair, or gardening, if the discussion comes up, just sit there and listen. To stay in interesting, you can occasionally add "that's interesting," "fascinating," "amazing," or "that's great." you may, of course, ask questions to show interest, but the less said, the better. It is better that they think you are a fool than to open your mouth and remove all doubt!

You should try to gain acceptance and break the ice as soon as possible. This is a good skill to use when interviewing. It may be a set of golf clubs in the corner, a photo of an airplane on the wall, or a fishing trophy. This is a good and useful technique, but do not go into depth if you have none. You can show interest, but listen more than talk.

The Touch

It has been suggested that those who touch more are seen as having more charisma. With this mind, let's see how we can make touching work for you. The way we shake hands becomes another component of this search scenario. Yes, it is complex, because the way you shake hands can add to your Interview or become a very bad element.

Note

* What not to do when shaking hands!

* Do not be a Ring Squeezer or a McBone Crusher. No one likes a person who tries to show off by breaking a hand. This type of handshake could the door on you getting hired.

* The clam Hand or Mr. McFish shake. This limp handshake will send you limping out the door. The message here is a lack of self-confidence.

* The McPumper. The person that keeps cranking and pumping up and down. An other you're-out-the door exercises. You may think we are kidding, but we are not! Remember, the interviewer is looking for the best applicant and the best ap plicant is the one who they are most comfortable with. The pumper suggests fake enthusiasm and that means you are not sincere.

* Mr. McGlue Hand. This is very annoying. For a moment, think how you would feel if someone was holding on to you for a minute or so while they were trying to carry on a conversation. This is another kiss of death in scoring with the inter view.

* The McJerker. You know those who give you the one short "jerk" and quickly pull that hand away. This tells everyone that you couldn't care less about and you do not like people anyway. You can be assured that with this attitude this inter viewer does not want you on his team. You have no real chance of ever getting this job.

You should try to do a hand shake with your friends before you go in for the interview. This will help you to dry run things to see if there are any problems with how you do it. You must be able to do it at any time during the interview because someone may walk into the office while you are doing the interview.

As funny as it might sound, we want you to work with a friend and practice your handshake because this one physical touch can end your interview before it even begins.

Note: You may shake hands with a woman if you are a man, but let the interviewer offer her hand. This gives her an option of shaking your hand or not.

References

Make up a list of references you can give an employer if you are asked to do so. Your references should be old family friends. You should always call the reference to be sure they will be a reference for you. You want them to tell the employer that they know you and you would be a great employee. Do not let them tell anything except this.

One of our recent students give a reference and when the employer called him, he said, "Yes, he know that person; he stole his stereo." Needless to say, the student did not get the job.

Typical Bottom Line

Interview Questions

Instruction: Think about how your key concepts and
                      each R.A.C.E. You prepared will apply when
                      you are asked these or other questions. Remember
                      your "hook" or feedback question.

1. Why should we hire you?
2. Can you work under pressure, deadlines, etc.?
3. What is your greatest strength? Weakness?
4. How long would it take you to make a contribution to our firm?
5. How long would you stay with us?
6. What are your short-range objectives?
7. What do you look for in a job?
8. What is your philosophy of management?
9. Do you prefer staff or line work?, Why?
10. What kind of salary are you work?
11. What are your five biggest accomplishments in your present or last job?
Your career so far?
12. Why didn't you do better in college?
13. Why are you leaving? Why did your business fail?
14. What business, character and credit references can you give us?
15. What can you do for us that someone else cannot do?
16. How good is your health?
17. How do you feel about people from minority groups?
18. If you could start again, what would you do differently?
19. How doe you rate yourself as a professional? As an executive?
20. What new goals or objectives have you established recently?
21. How have you changed the nature of your job?
22. What do you think of your boss?
23. What is your feeling about: alcoholism? Divorce? homosexuals? Women in
    business? Religion? Abortion?

24. Why haven't you obtained a job so far?
25. What features of your previous jobs have you disliked?
26. Would you describe a few situations in which your work was criticized?
27. Would you object to working with a woman/man?
28. How would you evaluate your present firm?
29. Do you generally speak to people before they speak to you?
30. How would you describe the essence of success?
31. What was the last book you read? Movie you saw? Sporting event you attended, etc.?
32. In your present position, what problems have you identified that had previously been overlooked?
33. What interests you most about the position we have? The least?
34. Don't you feel you might be better off in a different size company? Different type company?
35. Why aren't you earning more at your age?
36. Will you be out to take your boss's job?
37. Are you creative? Give an example.
38. Are you analytical? Give an example.
39. Are you a good manager? Give an example.
40. Are you a leader? Give an example.
41. How would you describe your own personality?'
42. Have you helped increase sales? Profits? Reduce costs?
43. What do your subordinates think of you?
44. Have you fired people before?
45. Have you hired people before? What do you look for?
46. Why do you want to work for us?'
47. If you had your choice of jobs and companies, where would you go?
48. What other types jobs are you considering? What companies?
49. Why do you feel you have top management potential?
50. Tell us about yourself.

Interview Questions - Associate Principal

1. Tells about your experience and background that qualifies you for this position?
2. Explain how you would handle a teacher that was reported that he/she was not do his/her job as a teacher?

3. How would you handle a classified employee who was show up late daily for his/her job?

4. We are expecting a large number of inexperience teachers, how would you go about helping these teachers to be more effective in the classroom?

5. One of our major problems here at this high school is attendance, what would you do or suggest that would improve attendance?

6. We find that our test scores are low in English and Math, what would you suggest that would help to improve these scores.

7. Why do you want this position?

8. Do you have any questions of us?

Note: These are just a sampling of some of the questions that are asked an Associate Principal applicant.

Interview Questions - Teacher

1. Tells about your experience and background that qualifies you for this position?

2. If we came into your classroom what would we see?

3. Explain the various methods of discipline you employ in the classroom?

4. Are you willing to sponsor clubs? FBLA? VICA? Yearbook? Drill team? Other?

5. Can you coach a sport? Basketball? Track? Football? Swimming? Other?

6. How do you motivate your students to do their work?

7. Do you have experience working with cultural diverse students?

8. What classes would you prefer to teach?

Note: This is a sample of some of the questions ask a teacher applicant.

REFERENCES

From the Desk of Gene Merhish

October 31, 1995

Mr. & Mrs. Don Hess   Ernie Havner   Dan Stephens
240 Calvert Ct.   7912 Colgate Ave.   Protech Sys.
Santa Clara, CA 95051   Westminster, CA 92683   4035 Cheyenne Ct.
408-246-5643   Chino, CA 91710
                             714-894-7555
                                                        909-590-9521

Vern Thomason   Tom Mann   Bobby Kuhlmann
10844 Dryden   Unit 97, 15111 Pipeline Ave.
    Chaffey College
Cupertino, CA 95014   Lake Los Serrans   58885 Haven Ave.
408-446-1554   Chino, CA 91709   Rancho Cucamonga, CA
                             909-623-1700   909-987-1737

Roy S. Loo, Reg. VP   Sam Chebeir, Pres.   Cliff Thorn
Primamerica Fin. Serv.   Trans American Plastic   Ethan Allen
7201 Arlington Ave., Ste. 2 5601 East Santa Ana St.   14211 Monte Vista Ave.
Riverside, CA 92503   909-988-8555   909-591-6451
909-785-9346

Merlie L. Runolfson   Pat Russell   Toni Po Wok
Hayward Unified School Dist. 5001 Atherton Street, #401
    14578 Terrace Hill Ct.
Box 5000   Long Beach, CA 90815   Chino, CA
Hayward, CA 94540   310-597-2310   909-597-7152
415-881-2600

Jack Worthington   Jack Menzia, Prin.   Robert W. Demetter
2465 Quail Run   La Sierra HS   Van Air

192

Sandy, Utah 84092   4145 La Sierra Ave.   2950
Mechanic Street
801-942-2465   Riverside, CA 92505   Lake
City, PA 16423

                            909-351-9238   814-774-3482

Chapter Twenty-three

Multiple Party Interviews

There will be time when you are going to be interviewed by a panel or more than one person. We have faced this situation many times. You may be warned in advance and sometimes not. Your position here is that you should be prepared regardless of how many people are interviewing you. If possible, try to find out if it will be a group decision in hiring you or if there will be only one person making the decision on the job you are applying for.

You will be asked questions by many different people. Sometimes, there will be a lot of questions coming from all directions at the same time. Each panelist may ask questions from a formal list or extemporaneous questions. Answer all the questions quickly, briefly, and as accurate as you can. Do not try to fake answers. If you do not know the answer. State the that you do not the answer. Look in the directly at the person who is asking the question. Try to make direct eye contact with all of the panelist in turn.

In the Educational community you will find that the panelist arrangement of interview is common place. We have seen from 5-7 panel members. More often than not, each panelist will ask one question at a time in a sort of "round robin" scenario. In the business climate, more often than not, the interview will be one on one. Sometimes, there may be more than one person involved. On occasion, we have seen multiple interviews taking place in a restaurant where the author has interview the President and Vice President of a corporation.

A dispute may arise between people on the panel. You should give your opinion if you are asked. A dispute may arise over one of your answers. Do not get into an argument with anyone on the panel. If necessary, state you position, but if you argue, you will always lose. The panelists will always fee they are right. This will result in you possible not getting the job.

You should generally side with the top-ranked person on the panel if you can, but do not tell this person that he or she is wrong. He/she will probably be important in deciding if you get hired. You want him/her on your side. Some times he/she has the only say in who gets the job. Try to get him/her to like you.

Above all, always dress appropriately for the interview. We have discussed in more detail the appropriate dress.

Ask for feedback on your resume and presentation at the end of the interview. This may or may not happen, but if you do not ask, you can assured you will not get a critique of your work or presentation. This may help you to change something for your next interview that will make you "shine" that much brighter. Remember, there will always be another interview.

Always ask what the next step is until you are hired and what the time frame is for these steps. I, Bob Dussman, once interviewed at a company that was going to hire someone six (6) months in the future. This kind of situation can be a waste of your time and gas unless you are currently employed and looking toward the future for opportunities. You may want to find out when they are hiring before you go to the interview. This will avoid wasting your time and efforts over non job. Companies have been known to conduct interviews merely to poll the market to see what is available and at what price. These polling exercises are a waste of your time since they will never result in your getting a job because there is no job!!!

Attempting to get as much other information as possible out of the panel is always prudent. This may include things like how many jobs are available and how many people have applied for the various positions. The more information you have, the better off you are. Remember, information is "power." Ask how many people are ahead of you.

It is always important to be on time. You should try to get to your interview early. This allows you to "check out" some of the organizations dynamics and collect your thoughts. You should use the rest room to make any adjustments to your appearance before the interview.

It is good idea to be there at least 15 minutes early. Call if there is some reason you are going to be late. You should not be late to an interview. Under no circumstance you do not want to be late without calling. You should use your portable phone, or a phone booth if you are going to be late without question.

In Southern California, and we are sure in many other metropolitan areas there are ever changing traffic conditions on our highways, streets, and thoroughfares leaving early for a job interview will give you the opportunity to adjust to these conditions, as well as allow you to locate unfamiliar addresses. Besides, you need to find a parking place, your papers, and so on.

It is generally not a good idea to ask for or get coffee. There is a chance that in the process of moving from your seat to the interview that you might spill. This has happened to some with a "cola." This has happened to me Mr. Merhish, and as you can understand this can distract you from the interview and it has. You are attempting to clean up and do the interview.

Chapter Twenty-four

Follow-up Letter

After every interview, you need to send the interviewer a follow-up letter. This is designed to do two things. First, you need to express your appreciation for being allowed the time to interview. If, for some reason, the interviewer has not decided upon a finalist, this follow-up letter may help persuade the interviewer to at least select you for a sec- ond or third interview. A good follow-up letter can be an effective marketing tool if used correctly. It is hoped that, at this time, you have a better understanding abut the job you are interviewing for so now you can design this let- ter around this new information. It gets you name, ideas, and qualifi- cations in front of the interviewer and decision- maker again.

As an example, keep in mind that there may be more appli- cants than just you out there. Sometime ago, an applicant was interviewing for a management position with Sta- ples. The applicant was told that he was selected from 80 applicants for the initial interview. For the second interview, he was one of nine. There may be many times more applicants. So you want to take every opportunity to continue to sell your case, point out that your are the most valuable appli- cant. Each time that you talk to the employer, interviewer, or decision-maker, you will want to send a follow-up letter discussing what transpired during the interview and continue to sell the fact that you will be a benefit to the organization.

Try to give a brief review of what you thought the key points were in your last meeting. This may remind the interviewer who you are and what was discussed. It will at least keep you in the inter- viewer's mind. This is important. You should remember that old adage, "Out of sight, out of mind."

The following are some examples for follow-up letters. You should use these as guides only. You will want to write up your own follow-up letters.

CONFIDENTIAL INFORMATION

Name in full_____ Date;_____
     (Last)   (First)   (Middle)   Nick Name

Home Address:_____
     (Street and Number)   (Box Number)   (City)   (State)   (Zip)

                              HOME _____
Years at Present Address: _____   PHONE: (Area Code & Number)
                              BUSINESS_____
                                (Area Code & Number)

Date of Birth			Age		Height	Weight	Social Security Number:
Month	Day	Year	Years	Months			

Marital Status		Wedding Anniversary	Wife: Name & Birth Date		Children (Number)	Dependents (other than wife)
Single	Married					

Children: Name_____ Name_____
            (Birth Date)   (Birth Date)

          Name_____ Name_____
            (Birth Date)   (Birth Date)

YOUR PERSONAL BALANCE SHEET

Do you own your home? _____ Amount of mortgage _____ If you rent, your monthly rent _____

Do you own your funiture? _____ Do you own an automobile? _____
                                                Make & Model

Amount of Life Insurance _____ Present monthly living expenses _____
                                          (You and your family)

Other source of income while employed by us_____ Amount of such income _____
                                                   (Yearly)

If wife is employed state _____ and _____ Last Medical Exam. _____
              (occupation)   (amount of income)   (Date)

Loans or debts past due? (Other than home)_____ Total amount of such indebtedness:

$_____ . Your Bank _____.

REFERENCES

PERSONAL: Persons, other than relatives, you have known for five years or more......

_____ _____ _____
    (Name)   (Address)   (Occupation)

_____ _____ _____
    (Name)   (Address)   (Occupation)

BUSINESS: Firms you have been employed by or have had business dealings with ....
                              197

_____ _____ _____
    (Name)   (Address)   (Explain)

_____ _____ _____
    (Name)   (Address)   (Explain)

SALES   EXPERIENCE

Have you sold our type of products before? _____ or _____ For how long? _____
                                             (Yes)   (No)

For whom: _____ _____
                    (Name)   (Location)

Please summarize any other sales experience you may have had:

Product _____ For _____ Years _____

Product _____ For _____ Years _____

Product _____ For _____ Years _____

List below the territories which you have worked for a year or more:

_____

_____

What territories do you feel you know best and why? _____

_____

Specify and explain your preference with respect to territory assignment: _____

_____

Which of your assets (background, education, territory knowledge, etc.) do you feel would be
most valuable in your association with us: _____

_____

Explain briefly why you are attracted to this type of business and an association with our
company: _____

_____

In case of emergency, notify: _____
                                  (Name)   (Address)   (Phone)

Physical Handicaps: _____

IMPORTANT: READ AND SIGN AT BOTTOM

It is my understanding that I will work at my own discretion at such time as I wish for the best
and maximum production. Schaeffer Mfg. Company will have no control over the time when I
conduct these sales.

DATE: _____   Signature _____

SCHAEFFER MFG.¹⁹⁸ COMPANY

102 Barton Street   St. Louis, Missouri 6310

FORM S-2000

EMPLOYMENT APPLICATION

Personal Information

Date of application ____/____/____

Name (Last) _____ (First)
(Middle)   Social Security No.

_____

_____
Home address
City   State
Zip

_____

_____
Home Telephone
Business Telephone   May we contact you
at work?
(   )
(   )
(   ) Yes   (   ) No
Position Applying For:_____ Days and hours
Day Mon Tues Wed Thur Fri Sat Sun
                                available. Com-
Date available:_____ plete if
applying From_____
                                for restaurant
Are you interested in (check all that apply):
    position.   To_____
 ( ) Full-time   ( ) Part-time   ( ) Temporary   ( )
Summer_____
Are you willing to relocate? If you are under 18 years of
    Are you willing to travel?
( ) Yes   ( ) No   age, please state your
date   ( ) Yes   ( ) No
                    of birth _____
                    (No one under age 16 may be hired) What
percent?_____%

_____

_____
How were you referred to this company?

_____

_____
Education_____

_____
Type of   Degree/Area
Number of   Graduated

School of Study	Name and Location of School Years Attended	(Check one)

High
Yes   No
School
State
(   )   (   )

_____

_____

Name   Address

College
Yes   No

        City   State
Zip   (   )   (
)

_____

_____

Name   Address

Graduate
Yes   No
School   City
State   Zip
(   )   (   )

_____

_____

Name   Address

Other
Yes   No
        City   State
Zip   (   )   (
)

_____

_____

```
U.S. Military
Service_____

_____Branch of Service          Technical
Specialization      Rank Attained_____

_____

_____
Special
Skills_____

_____
Typing Speed     Shorthand or Speed writing     CRT
PC Software/Other Equipment
_____wpm                    _____wpm
_____(Strokes/Hour)

_____

_____
Legal_____

Are you a U.S. citizen?  (  ) Yes    (  ) No   If no, do you
have a legal right & necessary documents to
work in the U.S.?  (  ) Yes    (  ) No   (Identity and
employment eligibility of all new hires will be verified
as required by the Immigration  Reform and Control Act of
1986.)

Were you ever discharged by any company?  (  ) Yes    (  ) No
If yes, give name of company(ies).

_____

_____

Reason for
discharge_____

_____

Have you even been convicted of a crime other than a minor
traffic violation?  (  ) Yes    (  ) No   If yes, please
explain offense and final disposition:

_____

_____

_____

_____

_____

_____
```

Employment
History_____

_____
List employment starting with your most recent position.
Account for any time during this period
that you were unemployed by stating the nature of your
activities. May we contact your present
employer? ( ) Yes   ( ) No   Past employer? ( ) Yes   (
) No   Please indicate if you were employed
 under a different
name._____

_____
                                    Position Held
List Major   Salary   Reason For
Dates   Name and Address of Employer
and Supervisor   Duties   or Wages
Leaving__
From: Name
Your Job Title   Starting
___/___   _____
mo. yr.   Address   City
State   _____
To: _____
Supervisor   Final
___/___   Phone
mo. yr.   (
)_____
From: Name
Your Job Title   Starting
___/___   _____
mo. yr.   Address   City
State   _____
To: _____
Supervisor   Final
___/___   Phone
mo. yr.   (
)_____

_____

From: Name
Your Job Title   Starting
___/___ _____
mo. yr.   Address   City
State   _____
To: _____
Supervisor   Final
___/___   Phone
mo. yr.   (
)_____

From: Name
Your Job Title   Starting
___/___ _____
mo. yr.   Address   City
State   _____
To: _____
Supervisor   Final
___/___   Phone
mo. yr.   (
)_____
_____

Have you previously worked for this company or any of its

subsidiaries or franchisees? ( ) Yes ( ) No
Name _____
Location_____
City and State _____ Position Held

Supervisor _____ Dates Employed:
From_____ To _____
Reason for leaving

_____
__
_____

References-

_____
Business references: (Do not list relatives.) (Indicate if
you were employed under a different name.)__
Name   Address   Work Phone
Title   Years Known
                         (
)_____

_____ (
)_____
_____ (
)_____
_____
_____
Please read
carefully_____
_____

In submitting this application for employment, I understand
that an investigation may be made
whereby information is obtained regarding my character,
previous employment, general reputation, educational
background, credit record and/or criminal history. I
authorize anyone possessing this information to furnish it
to _____ and/or a 3rd party company upon
request and I
release anyone so authorized, _____, and any
3rd party company for all liability
and damages whatsoever in furnishing, obtaining or using
said information.

In the event of employment, I understand that false or
misleading information given in my application
or interview(s) may result in immediate dismissal. I
understand, also, that I am required to abide by all rules
and regulations of_____.

I understand and agree that if employed, the employment will
be "at will." That is, either I or the
company may end the employment relationship at any time, for
any reason, or for no reason. I
understand that receipt of this application by the company
does not imply employment and that this application and/or
any other company documents are not contracts of
employment._____

Applicant's signature: _____
Date signed: _____

EMPLOYMENT APPLICATION

__Date of Application_

Month   Day   Year

_____

*   It is the company's policy to provide equal
opportunity in conformance with all applicable laws.
*   In accordance with the Immigration Reform and Control
Act of 1986, any offer of employment is
         conditioned upon satisfactory proof of applicant's
identity and legal ability to work in the U.S.

PERSONAL

_____

Name: Last   First
Middle   Social Security Number   Home
Phone

_____
-_____-_____(   )_____
Address
City   State   Zip Code
Daytime/Message

_____
_____(_____)_____
Are You Under The Age Of 18? Yes _____   No _____
       Can You Submit Proof Of Age? Yes _____   No _____

_____

Name/Address/Phone Number Of Person To Contact In Case Of
Emergency

_____

_____

EMPLOYMENT
DESIRED_____

What Type Of Work Are You Interested In?
Wage Desired?

_____

Are You Currently Employed? _____   If So, May We
Contact Your Present Employer?

Yes _____   No _____

Yes _____   No _____

_____

_____

Are There Any Hours, Shifts, Or Days You Cannot   If
Yes, When:

Or Will Not Work?   Yes _____   No _____

_____

_____

Date Available For Employment: Do You

Have Adequate Transportation To Get To Work?

Yes _____

No _____

_____

_____

GENERAL
INFORMATION _____

Have You Ever Worked For This Company Previously?   If
Yes, When: Where:
                          Yes _____   No _____

_____

Supervisor's Name: _____   Reason For Leaving:

_____

Are You Able To Perform All The Essential Functions Of The
Job With Or Without Reasonable Accommodations For
Which You Are Applying?   Yes _____   No _____

_____

Have You Been Convicted Of A Felony?   If Yes, Please
Explain.   When? _____
Yes _____   No _____   Where? _____
Action Taken? _____

_____

If Hired, Do You Agree To Abide By The Safety Rules
     If Hired, Can You Provide Proof Of Eligibility To Work
In
Of The Company?   Yes _____   No _____
     The U.S. Prior To Starting Work? Yes _____   No _____

_____

Have You Ever Been Counseled For Cash Handling Situations?
Yes _____   No _____
If Yes, Please Explain:

_____

_____

EDUCATION
HISTORY _____

School _____   Name & Location
         Major   Level Or Years   Type of Degree

_____ Completed ___   Or Certificate___
High
School _____

_____
Colleges/

Other Schools-
_____
_____

IDENTIFICATION
REQUIREMENTS_____
_____
The Immigration And Control Act Of 1986 Requires That If
Hired, Before You Start Work, You Present To
The Selecting Manager Documents Which Establish Your
Identity And Eligibility To Work In The
United States. Some Of The Documents Are:
*   United States Passport   *   Current Foreign
Passport With   *   Driver's License
*   Certificate Of Citizenship   Attached
Employment   *   State ID Card With
Photo
*   Certificate Of Naturalization
Authorization   *   U.S. Military Card
*   Alien Registration Card   *   Social Security Card
                *   U.S. Birth Certificate
     With
Photo_____
_____

EMPLOYMENT
HISTORY_____

Please Read Carefully: Begin With Present Or Most Recent
Employer And List All Jobs You Have Held For The Past Five
Years. Include Any Relevant Volunteer Work Experience.
Account For Periods Of Unemployment In The Space Provided
Below._____

_____

From: To: Employer's Name And Complete
Address (Company Name, Street No., City, State, Zip)
MO   YR   MO
YR_____

Starting Wage: Ending Wage: Your Job Title:
Immediate Supervisor: Telephone
$ PER $ PER

(   )_____
Description Of Duties:
_____

Reason For Leaving: May We
Contact? Yes _____   No _____
_____
_____

_____

From: To: Employer's Name And Complete
Address (Company Name, Street No., City, State, Zip)
MO   YR   MO
YR_____

Starting Wage: Ending Wage: Your Job Title:
Immediate Supervisor: Telephone
$ PER $ PER

(   )_____
Description Of Duties:
_____

Reason For Leaving: May We
Contact? Yes _____   No _____
_____
_____

EMPLOYMENT
HISTORY_____

Please Read Carefully: Begin With Present Or Most Recent
Employer And List All Jobs You Have Held For The Past Five
Years. Include Any Relevant Volunteer Work Experience.
Account For Periods Of Unemployment In The Space Provided
Below._____

_____

From: To: Employer's Name And Complete
Address (Company Name, Street No., City, State, Zip)
MO   YR   MO
YR_____

Starting Wage: Ending Wage: Your Job Title:
Immediate Supervisor: Telephone
$ PER $ PER

(   )_____
Description Of Duties:
_____

Reason For Leaving: May We
Contact? Yes _____   No _____
_____
_____

_____

From: To: Employer's Name And Complete
Address (Company Name, Street No., City, State, Zip)
MO   YR   MO
YR_____

Starting Wage: Ending Wage: Your Job Title:
Immediate Supervisor: Telephone
$ PER $ PER

(   )_____
Description Of Duties:
_____

Reason For Leaving: May We
Contact? Yes _____   No _____
_____
_____

From: _____ To: _____ Employer's Name And Complete
Address (Company Name, Street No., City, State, Zip)
MO   YR   MO
YR _____

_____
Starting Wage: Ending Wage: Your Job Title:
Immediate Supervisor: Telephone
$ PER $ PER

(   ) _____
Description Of Duties:

_____
Reason For Leaving: _____   May We
Contact? Yes _____   No _____

_____

_____

_____

Please Explain Any Periods Of
Unemployment: _____
_____

From: _____ To: _____ How Did You Spend
your Time? _____

From: _____ To: _____ How Did You Spend
your Time? _____

_____

_____

DRUG AND ALCOHOL
POLICY_____

The Company Has A Vital Interest In Maintaining A Drug And
Alcohol Free Environment For Its Employees, Customers
And Visitors. Therefore, The Company Prohibits The Use Of,
Possession Of, Distribution Of, Purchase Or Sale Of,
Offering To Purchase Or Sell, Transfer Of, Trafficking In,
And Working Or Reporting For Work Under The Influence Of
Intoxicants, Drugs Or Controlled Or Illegal Substances.
Applicants For Employment May Be Required To Take And Pass
A Drug And Alcohol Screening Test Before They Can Begin To
Work And Employees May Be Tested If The Company
Has A Reasonable Suspicion Of Substance Abuse. Results Of
Such Tests Will Be Kept Confidential In Accordance With
Applicable Laws. _____

_____

PLEASE READ AND SIGN
BELOW_____

I Hereby Certify That The Information Contained In This
Application Form Is True And Correct To The Best Of My
Knowledge And Agree To Have Any Of The Statements Checked By
The Company Unless I Have Indicated To The
Contrary. I Authorize The References Listed Above To
Provide The Company With Any And All Information
Concerning My Previous Employment And Any Pertinent
Information That They May Have. Further, I Release All
Parties And Persons From Any And All Liability For Any
Damages That May Result From Furnishing Such Information
To The Company As Well As From The Use Or Disclosure Of Such
Information By The Company Or Any Of Its Agents,
Employees, Or Representatives. I Understand That Any
Misrepresentation, Falsification, Or Material Omission Of
Information On This Application May Result In My Failure To
Receive An Offer, Or, If I Am Hired, In My Dismissal
From Employment.

In Consideration Of My Employment, I Agree To Conform To The
Rules And Standards Of The Company And Agree
That My Employment And Compensation Can Be Terminated At
Will, With Or Without Cause, And With Or Without
Notice, At Any Time, Either At My Option Or At The Option Of
The Company._____

Applicant's Signature

_____ Date
_____

213

Chapter Twenty-five

The Follow-up Letter

After every interview, you need to send the interviewer a follow-up letter. This is designed to do two things. First, you need to express your appreciation for being allowed the time to interview. If, for some reason, the interviewer has not decided upon a finalist, this follow-up letter may help persuade the interviewer to at least select you for a sec- ond or third interview. A good follow-up letter can be an effective marketing tool if used correctly. It is hoped that, at this time, you have a better understanding abut the job you are interviewing for so now you can design this let- ter around this new information. It gets you name, ideas, and qualifi- cations in front of the interviewer and decision- maker again.

As an example, keep in mind that there may be more appli- cants than just you out there. Sometime ago, an applicant was interviewing for a management position with Sta- ples. The applicant was told that he was selected from 80 applicants for the initial interview. For the second interview, he was one of nine. There may be many times more applicants. So you want to take every opportunity to continue to sell your case, point out that your are the most valuable appli- cant. Each time that you talk to the employer, interviewer, or decision-maker, you will want to send a follow-up letter discussing what transpired during the interview and continue to sell the fact that you will be a benefit to the organization.

Try to give a brief review of what you thought the key points were in your last meeting. This may remind the interviewer who you are and what was discussed. It will at least keep you in the inter- viewer's mind. This is important. You should remember that old adage, "Out of sight, out of mind."

The following are some examples for follow-up letters. You should use these as guides only. You will want to write up your own follow-up letters.

Gene Merlush
984 La Paz Road Placentia, CA 92870

Wednesday, July 29, 1998

Dr. Kirt Harper
Santa Ana Unified School District
1601 East Chestnut Ave
Santa Ana, CA 92701-6322

Re: Teaching in your Horizon Program

Dear Kirt:

I want to take this moment to thank you for the time you and your colleagues spent with me discussing employment opportunities with the Santa Ana Unified School District. Also, assure that I enjoyed our meeting and conversation.

If you select me to teach in you district, I will bring the following attributes, experiences, and benefits:

- I am a fully qualified Business Education teacher.
- Experienced working with at "Risk" students.
- Over ten (ten) years of teaching experience at all levels: High School, Junior High School, Junior College, University, and Adult.
- Operated a Demonstration Program for Hayward Unified School District, ROC/P, and was recognized by the State of California Department of Business Education.
- Instructor for the U. S. Air Forde Reserves.
- Outstanding Student of the Year, Western Wyoming Junior College.
- Student Body President, Western Wyoming Junior College.
- Worked with disadvantaged and culturally diverse students.
- Taught in two (2) Juvenile Court Programs, Riverside County Department of Education and Orange County Department of Education.
- Taught in four (4) Junior Colleges.
- Taught in six (6) Adult Education Programs.

215

714-996-4221

- Hold California Service credential.
- Hold four (4) California Teaching credentials and two (2) Utah teaching credentials.
- Computer trained and competency.
- Taught Special Education and have some formal training.
- Administrative training.
- World traveled
- Flexible and a team player

I would extremely enjoy the opportunity to teach in the Santa Ana Unified School District, and I look forward to talking to you in the near future.

You may reach me at 714-996-4421

Sincerely,

Gene Merhish, AA, BS, & MA
GM/gm
Teach#1

Santa Ana Unified School District
1601 East Chestnut Ave.
Santa Ana, CA 92701-6322

Dear Kirt:

I want to take this moment to thank you for taking the time
to talk to me on the phone Tuesday, August 11, 1998.

I understand your concern about communicating with parents.
However, as I pointed out, I have been working with
culturally diverse students since 1972. Plus, last year I
operated and developed a program that was identified as
"SWIFT," School With a Future, a program designed for
students who were truant, educationally handicapped, and who
had behavior problems.

I worked very closely with parents to maintain contact,
indicate behavior, student attendance and report progress.
The results were very positive, and many parents were
pleased with the improvement of their students. I have
little to no problem communicating with parents and getting
their cooperation.

Students were assessed using pre and post ITAS testing.
Objectives and academic needs were adjusted to meet the
needs of each student.

The program also included self-awareness, conflict
resolution and peer mediation. We also worked on listening
skills, critical thinking, and problem-solving.

In addition, I was involved in a program called "Links."
This is a district-wide program to reduce violence, fights,
assaults, suspensions, and expulsions.

Furthermore, I have operated an award-winning program for
Hayward Unified School District, which was a demonstration
program for the State of California. Also, I was a Business
Education Consultant for the State of California.

I have also taught at all levels including five (5) adult
education programs, four (4) junior colleges, and at the
University level. Plus, I taught a "GAIN" & GED program at
the adult level for Colton School District.

I have about fifteen (15) years experience in the Military and have been a military instructor. I also bring approximately twenty-six (26) years of industrial and business experience.

As a "bonus," I will bring to Santa Ana Unified School District tens of thousands worth of computers and related equipment.

As I indicated, I am very interested in teaching and/or working at Santa Ana Unified School District. If you can at all use my skills or know of any other program that could benefit by my Business, Industrial, and Educational experience, please have someone contact me.

You may reach me almost everyday from 0800 to 1800 hours. Please call me at 714-996-4221.

Sincerely,

Gene Merhish, MA

"FOLLOW-UP" LETTER
SENT WITHIN 24 - 48 HOURS AFTER EACH MEETING

DATE

ADDRESSEE

Dear

I want to express my appreciation for the time and consideration you extended to me during our meeting on (DAY AND DATE). Following our meeting, I took the opportunity to review our discussion.

I am excited about my potential association with (NAME OF COMPANY, ORGANIZATION OR FIRM) and my interest and enthusiasm continue to be high. It seemed to me that the qualifications I possess are a good match with the specifications for the position. Important strengths which we discussed include:

* REMINDER TO IDENTIFY SPECIFIC AREAS OF IMPORTANCE ONLY: I.E. THE THREE (3) MAJOR RESPONSIBILITIES, SUBJECTS OR TOPICS DISCUSSED DURING THE MEETING.

* INCLUDE ONLY THOSE THINGS THAT SEEM TO BE MOST CRITICAL AND IMPORTANT TO THE INTERVIEWER FOR YOUR SUCCESS IN THE POSITION.

* KEEP IN MIND THEIR REQUIREMENTS FOR THE POSITION, NOT YOURS.

(The following paragraph must be modified to match the outcome of the meeting.)

I will be contacting you (AS DISCUSSED DURING THE MEETING - DAY OR DATE OR BY PHONE, WHICHEVER APPLIES) and look forward to a positive response or establishing the time and place of our next meeting.

Sincerely,

Sunday, March 15, 1998

Mr. Bruce F. Reichenfeld, Vice President
West Coast Rubber Machinery
P.O. Box 2159, 7180 Scout Ave.
Bell Gardens, California 90201

Re: Position of Responsibility Sales, Marketing Manager
and/or VP Sales

Dear Bruce:

I was delighted we had the opportunity to meet Saturday,
March 14, 1998, and this letter and enclosures are a
response to your interest in me to fulfill future managerial
requirements for your firm.

My purpose: to encourage you to initiate an action that
will enable me to meet with you in the near future to
further discuss opportunities with your firm.

My objective: to quickly relate my experience, skills, and
capacity to accept and respond to significant, continuing
responsibility (requirements you may be looking for in
staffing as you move your company forward).

I have functioned as
Sales/Marketing/Manager/Educator/Trainer in companies
requiring above average dedication and effort in order to
achieve desired results. In the course of meeting company
objectives, I have identified and improved upon
opportunities that resulted in increased market share and
profitable sales growth.

You may be interested in the following:

*   1987 System Salesman of the Year Top Territory of the
Year. Increased sales by   169 percent at times.
*   1986, 1987, and 1988 Managed a Million dollar sales
territory as salesman.
*   1991 as a Manager, developed National sales force and
increased marketing   penetration. Increased target

 Marketing and sales force training. Worked nationally and internationally.

*   As a General Manager, maintained gross profits over 75%
UNICO rotary repair   company.
*   I have experience in sales, advertising, and marketing
of "High Tech" Relays & Switches, Compressed Air Systems,
Hydraulic Systems, Machine Guarding,   Plastics, Stampings,
and Engineered products at the National level. For
companies   like Gardner-Denver, Proctor and Gamble, P &
H, Sullair, Quincy, and Joy.
*   Over ten (10) years experience (Systems Engineering)
working on jet aircraft, also   Missiles and Spacecraft.
*   Sales Manger for several companies in the sales of
Engineered products and have hands-on engineering
experience.
*   Consultant for the Department of Business Education,
State of California,   Distributive Education by Brenton
R. Aikin, Chief Bureau of Business   Education.
*   Worked with large complex customers.
*   I employ "GUERRILLA" marketing tactics to get the job
done!

*   Planned and managed: Developed, directed, client
interaction, trained, sales growth strategies, solution
selling, sales closure assistance, field sales support,
        and motivated, interfaced with independent sale
organization and distributors in a   number of industries
and markets nationally.

Conducted seminars, set goals, and orchestrated many
industrial shows nationally. Also budgeting, forecasting
and administration.

The enclosed resume will support the above and more. An
exploratory meeting with me will confirm it!

Although I would like to call you next week to determine if
a meeting can be scheduled, I believe that to be impractical
and disruptive. Rather than take up your time with repeated
phone calls, please call me to arrange a meeting at your
convenience. I am available for interview after 3:00 p.m.
everyday. And I will be available for employment after June
17, 1998 on a full-time or consulting basis. You may reach
me at 714-996-4221.

Thank you for your consideration

Sincerely

Gene Merhish, AA, BS, & MA
GM/gm - 9:11:43 AM

Enclosure

Samples of Other Letters

Thank You for Interview

Your Address

Inside Address
(If possible, use individual's name.)

Dear _____:

I appreciated the opportunity to talk with you on (date). The information you shared with me about (company name) was excellent, and I am excited about the possibility of applying my education and experience to the position we discussed.

If I can provide you with any additional information, please let me know. I look forward to hearing from you soon.

Sincerely,

(Written signature)

Your name typed

Thank You for Plant/Office Visit

Your Address

Inside Address
(If possible, use individual's name.)

Dear _____:

Thank you for your letter of (date) suggesting a plant/office visit at (time) on the following dates: (list dates).

The most convenient date for me would be (date). I will arrive at your office at (time).

Enclosed is a copy of my resume, along with the application for employment. (If necessary.)

I appreciate the opportunity to visit your plant/office. I am very interested and eager to learn more about possible employment opportunities with (organization name).

Sincerely,

(Written signature)

Your name typed

Letter of Acceptance

Your Address

Inside Address
(If possible, use individual's name.)

Dear _____:

I am very pleased to accept your offer <u>(state offer)</u> as outlined in your letter of <u>(date)</u>. (Include all details of offer—location, starting salary, starting date.)

(Mention enclosures—application, resume, employee forms, or other information—and any related commentary.)

I look forward to meeting the challenges of the job and I shall make every attempt to fulfill your expectations.

Sincerely,

(Written signature)

Your name typed

Letter of Rejection

Your Address

Inside Address
(If possible, use individual's name.)

Dear _____:

After considerable thought, I have decided not to accept your offer of employment as outlined in your <u>(date)</u> letter. This has been a very difficult decision for me. However, I feel I have made the correct one for this point in my career.

Thank you for your time, effort, and consideration. Your confidence in me is sincerely appreciated.

Sincerely,

(Written signature)

Your name typed

223

Chapter Twenty-six

How To Ask For Money

Normally, money and benefits are discussed in the second or third interview. But bear in mind, is not a team sport, and the rules are in the hands of the interviewer. And remember, the interviewer is looking for the best candidate. It could be the lowest, and most of the time not the highest, but surely an employee that can make decisions and negotiate in a positive manner will be considered.

If you are worth your "salt" at all, you must have a figure in mind. The employer believes that you have a value and that is why you were asked for a price for your services. You will confirm his/her belief by quoting an amount. We would suggest that you have a high and a rock bottom. Be in a position to negotiate. It would be prudent of you to be aware of what the industry is doing as well as the company's competition. If you can, try to find out the salary range of the job you are interviewing for in advance. Both county, state, and federal government, school districts, post salaries for most jobs. The department of employment in your state can provide you with some help in this matter. Also the

well as the with job announcements that not only give the job description, are researching everyone you ful.

county, state, federal agencies, as school districts will provide you nouncements that not only give the but state salary ranges. When you other prospective employers, ask come in contact with. But be tact-

Large corpora- with starting pay

tions may provide job descriptions as we stated the public sector does.

In the public sec- by for any public the educational to negotiation come later when and years of ex-

tor, all pay information is available job. This is true as we indicated for community, therefore, there is little with the interviewer. This may you are presenting your credentials perience.

There may be other times when salaries are not negotiable, namely, when there is a set wage for the position. If this is the case, the interviewer will most likely volunteer the information without questioning by the interviewee.

We would suggest that you approach the question of salary this way. "Based upon my background and experience, I believe that I am worth a starting salary of $_____."

Another approach would be, "I would suggest a starting range of $_____ to _____." But you could include, " I would be willing to entertain an offer that you feel best meets your needs." On the lines below, we would like you to develop a statement that best presents how you feel about what you should get paid. As we have said, being prepared make you a more qualified candidate.

_____
_____
_____
_____
_____
_____

You may find it hard to get salary information during the pre-interview visit. You may also seek out the Occupational Outlook Handbook. Read all the information on the occupation you intend to go after, then you are in a good position to answer any questions about your starting salary.

If you are trying to change fields, you may want to forget about holding out for a given salary. You will want to concentrate on the more desirable job, getting your foot in the door. When we moved back into education, we had been away for some time, Even with years of teaching experience, we were forced to accept about have what we had been making in indus- try. But like you, we were "downsized." We swallowed our pride and took the job. We knew once in, we could get current experience and move up the ladder. We are doing well, teaching at the University, Junior College, and the high school levels and are gaining recognition in the industry. One of our colleague faced the same experience. He had the degrees but was lacking the proper credentialing. He had to bite the "bullet" and take a major pay re- duction. But he got his foot in the door. We are not suggesting "pie in the sky," some-

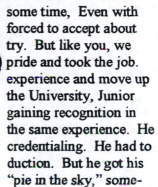

thing we have not faced. If you are in a dream job, something that you always have wanted, you may want to work for little as an "intern" to get you in the door.

Now we know that some of this is impractical. Many of you, like us, have families, house payments, and the rest. Just make sure that if you make such a commitment, the employer is the kind you would care to work for year after year, and one who will reward your ambition and your effort.

You can accomplish this, but you will need to do a thorough research. Count on spending more time than you would examining an ordinary employer. You want to make very sure you are making the right move. Always check your plan every few years to see if you are on track or have been derailed. Find out why if you have been derailed. Your authors keep a small notebook in our business bag or attaché case. Within this notebook you would find various goals, short and long-term. It may be here within your notebook that you have laid out your plan as we have and do.

Chapter Twenty-seven

If You Have Sold Yourself!

(When you are sure that the organization is interested in you, now you can ask your questions. This only when you are in a position to do your negotiation.)

Often at the end of the interview, the interviewer will ask you if you have any questions. So if you have gotten and evaluated the above signals positively, you can proceed with some-thing like this : "I am extremely in-terested in the position we have been discuss-ing, but before I can throw all to the wind and accept the position, I would like to ask you're a few question."

By the way, if you have asked good, solid, intelligent, well thought-out ques-tions, you have enhanced the probability of getting the position. The interviewer will think you are stupid if you do not ask good ques-tions.

Following are some questions that you may want to ask:

1. Is this a new position?
2. Over the last few years, has there been a high turnover in this position?
3. Is the person who was in this position still with the company? Is there any way I can talk with him/her?
4. What are the possibilities of promotions within the company if I do a good job?
5. What problems need to be solved with this positions?
6. May I see the job description for this position.
7. How many hours per week will I be required to work if I accept this position?
8. In your opinion, what is the future of the company?
9. In your opinion, do you believe that most employees are happy working here at the company?
10. What is the possibility of relocation?
11. To whom do I report? Will I have more than one boss?
12. Does the company face any serious problems of competition?
13. In the near future do you expect that the firm will be sold?

14. Is there anything else I can answer about my ability to handle this position?
15. When would you expect me to come to work if I am selected for the position?
16. Is this a permanent position?
17. Is there paid overtime?

If you have additional questions that you feel are important to your employment, write them down on the lines below. Remember, try to cover everything you feel you should know.

_____
_____
_____
_____
_____
_____
_____
_____
_____
_____
_____
_____
_____
_____
_____
_____
_____

Sell Yourself First!

Often applicants will start off their interview by asking what the company can do for them — pay, vacations, and so forth. By doing this, they are "showing themselves the door." Like a salesman, you are selling yourself in the interview. You are the "product." This is what we tell all our students. In selling products, you sell "benefits, " so when selling yourself, guess what? That's right, you sell benefits. You tell them exactly what you can do for them first!

Hopefully you have learned this by now, but try to be a good listener. Answer the interviewer's questions, then look for clues that indicate that the interviewer has an interest in hiring you. You should offer benefits and create interest and desire.

Did You Sell Yourself Well?

The following will give you some idea if there is an interest in you and that you have done a good job of selling yourself:

- If the interviewer states, "You remind me of my myself."
- When the interviewer calls other employees within the firm to come in the office to see you.
- If he/she proceeds to sell you the organization as hard as you were trying to sell yourself.
- If the interviewer shows you that he/she has become comfortable in talking to you.
- If he/she offers to take you on a tour of the company and starts to introduce you to members of the organization as you go around.
- If the interview starts to get long, running longer than thirty minutes.
- If you are asked, "when can you start work?"
- If the interviewer starts to go into details explaining the fringe benefits of the company.
- If the interviewer starts to discuss what level of remuneration you would need to accept employment.
- When he/she starts to discuss promotions after you have been working for the company for awhile.

The Closing Of The Interview

At the end of any good sales presentation (and interviewing for a job is a "sales presentation"), remember you are selling the most important product that you will ever have to sell—you. At some point, you will want to ask for order, or in this situation, ask for the job.

It is understood by the interviewer that most likely the best applicant for the job is the one who demonstrates she/she really wants the job. So if you believe that his is the position that you really want, then go after it. Tell the interviewer with conviction.

On the lines below, develop your own closing statement that will convince that interviewer that your want the position.

_____
_____
_____
_____
_____
_____
_____
_____
_____
_____

What To Say If You Do Not Want The Job!

As you are out there looking for that "dream Job," every now and again you are going to come upon a position that has the elements that do not meet your needs. Remember, you do not have to take any job that comes along. If you run into such a job, simply say, "Thank You, I appreciate the time you have given me." Always be warm and friendly. Even if this is not the position for you, the person who just interviewed you could become a good "networking" contact.

You Are Offered A Job, But You Are Not Sure!

In this case, you will want to be warm and friendly, thank the interviewer for the offer, then state that you want to give the offer serious thought. State that you would like a few days to make sure that there are no doubts and that you can do the best job possible. Suggest, "May I get back to you in a few days, say Tuesday or Wednesday?" Tell what you think is wrong with the current offer. Be honest.

You Are Rejected In The Interview?

Most people take a rejection personally. If you are turned down for that job you really wanted, you will be disappointed. However, do not show anger or resentment. You need to use your common sense and show that you are a mature individual. Leave the interview with class. As we suggested a few moments ago, the interview can become valuable for "networking" people. You may not get this job, but there may be another job and opportunity within the organization that better fits your education and experience. In addition, the interviewer might be able to put in a good word for you at another company. Always leave the door open. Remember that the person who got the job may quit. You may be the next person in line. Leave on good terms. Do not burn your bridges! You never know when you may need them.

What If You Are Delayed In Finding That "Dream Job?"

Do not panic or give up seeking that job that you really want. Remember, looking for a job is a "real" job. In fact, you should make sure that you put in 6 to 8 hours a day working on your plan and doing your job search. The hardest job you will ever have is to find a job.

Let me assure you that I have been down this road. I, Gene Merhish, can personally tell the story that at one time I was "five minutes from being homeless." That's right! Here is the thing. You do not want to accept that second or third rate job because this is what can happen. I have taken a couple of second rated jobs and the next thing you find, you are not being paid. Now you are worse off than you were. You are working to make someone else richer and not looking for a job that will get your career going. As a word to the wise, I have couple of companies out there at this writing that owe me thousands. Do not go on this road!

You might be able to use your ingenuity to create a business for yourself. Organize your skills in such a manner so that you sell them. The hardest thing is to find a qualified buyer! There are many occupations which can be marketed by an individual. Design some service on paper, develop a list of prospective customers, and advertise to them by newspaper, flyer, personal visit, or by phone. I, Gene Merhish, have used advertising and marketing skills to work for a Chinese restaurant, cleaners, and a chiropractor. So guess what? I got my cleaning done at "no charge," got to eat two meals a day, seven days per week, and also got some cash. I also substitute taught and taught part-time at the junior college level. My co-author worked in a law office, substituted, and had a few other odd jobs. No one gets rich without work unless you are very lucky.

Chapter Twenty-eight

Search Costs

Let's talk about the costs of job search for a moment or two. First, job search is a job, and a costly one at that. It can often be a full-time job or should be as we have discuss if you are out of work. It is most important thing there is if you want to survive in our complex society. You should spend up to 8 hours per day, six days per week. You may also want to set aside some time and as well how much money your willing to spend. Let's say that you want to send out 100 pieces of mail per week.

A good paper resume will cost up to $.08 per sheet. We put an average of 3 sheets in one envelope. Just this level alone is $64.00 per week which includes the envelop and postage. You may have to spend more than $300 a month when you include the colored newsletter. There are other costs associated with the search. The cost for ink, phone calls, transportation, faxing, and more. A good job search program isn't an inexpensive task.

Let us share some additional thoughts about the cost of a job search campaign. We have a longtime friend of about thirty years. He was employed by a world renowned aerospace firm. We was "downsized" about a year ago or so. His approach to job search was to mail out perhaps 5 resumes per weeks or less. On the other hand, When one of authors was downsized he was mailing 25 to 30 resumes a day. Hence, many times the cost. As we have found out, it takes more than 100 resumes mailed to generate and interview our work is cut out for us. As the title of the book indicated, there was a point that over 7,001 resumes were sent out. During the recession of the early 90's there were ten's of thousands of Americans competing for very few jobs. Today, with the economy "booming", there are still thousands out there looking for good jobs and upward mobility. The point is, it is still competitive.

Take your time and set up a job search budget that works for you and meets your exportations. Do not forget your only going to get out a job search program what you put in it. As the old saying goes " Nothing ventured nothing gained." So if finding a job is important to you, do not take it likely, and do not under estimate its cost. Also remember that whatever the cost is your goal is always the same: to get a job. You will have to pay whatever the price is. You must be willing to sacrifice to get there. This is something only you can do. No one can do this work for you.

Whatever you do—do not quit!

If you are degreed, you can make money as a consultant, tutor, research analyst, tax preparer , bookkeeper, or with a variety of other business educational services. Or as we did, you might be able to substitute teach. Since it is projected that there will be a national shortage of teacher, this approach could offer a fair part-time position or a new career for you. Most states are looking for de-

greed indi- viduals as a minimum requirement. We would recommend, that you discuss the requirements for a teaching emergency
credential with any local School District or County Office of Education.

Specific vocational skills are even easier to market. There are
many small businesses that would be pleased to find a person
who per- forms clerical services at home as an example. Typing
and word processing can be an excellent source of income that
you can do from home. If you are skilled in the use of computers,
you might start a training program.

People in the health profession can make some reasonable amount of money working part time in the care of the aged, the handicapped, or home care.

You may look for additional sources of income by perhaps turn-pho-
ing your hobby into cash! You might be able to teach dance, un
tography, catering, art, or dog training. Do not leave any rock
turned. No mater what you elect, be sure you review your write
plans. Talk to others to see how they did it. Make sure you and
everything down. You are going to have to establish a budget
keep good records. We will discuss the reasons for this later. been

This is Mr. Merhish, one of the best part-time jobs that I have been
able to develop is the teaching of Marketing and Business
courses at the Junior Col-
lege and Graduate School. Not
only has it been financially beneficial but personally rewarding.
So if you have some special training it is possible to turn these
skills and experience into money.

Most importantly, do not get into the bad habit of putting things off.
Do not waste your time. If you procrastinate, it could cost you your
"dream job" and the balance of sources that might have. Remember to keep working until you get what you

want!

Chapter Twenty-nine

Tax Deduction Job Search

Because of your job search you may generate large expenses as a results. In most cases you will be able to deduct some if not all of your job search costs. This includes the cost of your car mileage to and from our interview. Also any related transportation costs. This includes picking up materials, copies from Office Max. Costs for postage, paper, ink, air fare, meals, and all associated costs. If you fax your resume, special deliver, or have any special preparation make sure you get and keep all receipts.

Develop the following list:

* Postage
* Paper cost/envelops
* Computer Ink
* Typing costs
* Mileage
* Gas expense
* Air fare
* Hotel costs
* Meals
* Phone and/or faxing
* Resume preparation
* Meals
* All associated job search cost

List here all cost associated to your job search:

_____
_____
_____
_____
_____

For further tax information on tax deductions, for job search please see your tax advisor or your CPA. This book is not intended to give you tax advice. These guidelines given are only to help you to evaluate your job search situation. Individual situations may vary.

Chapter Thirty

The Beginning Not The End!

To finally find a career position is not the end, it is only beginning of rebuilding a career. If you have made it to the end of the book, I hope your journey was rewarding. It was not too long ago that grand dad would work for a firm for thirty (30) years, receive the gold pocket watch, and retire. This story is happening less and less. We are not sure if it is a good or bad thing; but it is history for the most part today.

In my case, Gene Merhish, I have been in the Engineering field, Sales Field (many industries), Military, Educational

and not always be-
I was a "job hop-
look back and see
portunity. I have
nationally and also
No, I don't feel
around. However,
of work, and it was
So some of the
sary. I can assure
guy, according to
another story and

community at many levels, and more
cause I wanted to make a move or that
per." By the way, I hate that term. I
a lot of valuable experience and op-
worked with "key" people, traveled
have done some international work.
bad about changing jobs and moving
there were some times when I was out
a real battle getting my career going.
changing jobs was done out of neces-
you I like to eat as well as the next
my wife, maybe too much. That's
book.

The point is this: there are going to be some good times and bad. You will want to do your best to minimize the bad. You will want to do the best job of research you can to find the best job of research you can to find the best position that fits you and affords you the opportunity of career growth you are looking for. But today we would advise that you keep honing your skills and keep your resume up-to-date. The more you practice, the better you will get!

There are many out there who would suggest in today's global economy that your actively continue to keep looking for a job and interview any time and all the time you get the opportunity. This will keep your interviewing skills sharpened. Besides the fact that one day you will come upon the "job of your dreams." You should remember this dream job may prove to be a mirage if the organization changes. As you know, every time we pick up the newspaper, turn on the radio or TV, some major company is "downsizing," "restructuring," reorganizing," or "right-sizing;" it could be the firm that you are currently working for. We are not telling you to become "paranoid."

We are suggesting that you prepared. As late as yesterday, we were addressing a class of students explaining to them how today we will more than likely have several jobs in our career as well as several career paths. Because of this, plus the fact that technology is moving so quickly, We suggested

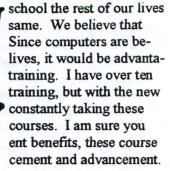

to them that we see ourselves going to and suggested that they plan on doing the this is a wise path for you to follow. coming more, and more a part of our geous that you take additional computer (10) years of computer experience and programs, come out all the time I am classes. Then there are Management are getting my drift. Besides the appar- are generally deductible as career in Han school the rest of our lives same. We believe that Since computers are be- lives, it would be advanta- training. I have over ten training, but with the new constantly taking these courses. I am sure you ent benefits, these course cement and advancement. You will need your tax consultant for details in this area.

Remember, find yourself a "champion." in fact, if you can, find a champion in several careers areas. This is not an easy task. It can be "prudent" on your part. You will never know when you are going to need someone to go to "bat" for you in your behalf. Also, "network, network, network." We can't overemphasize this point. This is at you place of business, church, club, and everywhere you go. We talk to everyone we can. We give them our business cards. This, the business card, is one of the best $10.00 to $30,00 investment you will ever make. You can use the business card from your firm. If you do not have a business card from your place of business or do not want to associate your firm with your job search, have your own personal business card made up. You can just have you name, address, and phone number, or offer some special service. Be creative. ALWAYS carry your business card with you. You should give it out freely to anyone who may help you on your job search. Since almost every restaurant has a "Free" lunch collection bowling you be able to pick-up a lunch once in while too.

Build yourself a job search portfolio or binder. In this portfolio, place samples of your various cover letters, resumes, applications, and other important documents that may be valuable in your job search mission. One of the classes we teach at the High School level includes this component project for the student to do. They complete the semester and have this tool that can be used in their career development and job search.

Many times you my be required to fill out a job application, provide references, letters of recommendation, if you are a teacher your placement file, or transcripts. Your portfolio, binder, or Job Search Handbook, will provide you with a central location to store and keep this information for quick reference. We also keep samples of some of our special work in our binder, such as Advertising material designs, and samples of newsletters. So are advice to you is to build your own binder, handbook, or portfolio it will be helpful in your job search.

If you start your own business as a career alternative, great, but do not try it alone. Seek out advice and talk to people in similar businesses that might be interested in. In other words, "do your research." if it means that you have to take special training, travel some distance to get the information, or invest a little money in the beginning, do it. Ask questions and opinions. Seek thoughts, suggestions and ideas. If you know what the business you are going to go into, be a great "listener" and write everything down.

When you have gotten an idea and it excites you by keeping you awake at night and on your mind all the time, you may want proceed. At this points, talk to business people in this industry, the manufactures, and then start developing a business and marketing plan. You will also want to talk to your banker, and more importantly your family. Often businesses fail because the family fails to buy into the development of the business. There are approximately 15 million small businesses in America, and over a million new ones start yearly, but only 10 percent make it beyond five years. So to give yourself and the business a better chance, follow the proven steps. Small businesses fail because of a lack of money. A lack of money caused solely by bad management. The scope of this book is not to prepare you to go into business, that is another book. But we will suggest, you seek out training and help from your local Community College, or Continuing Education Program. You may also feed courses at most Universities. In addition, you can obtain information from the U. S. Small Business Administration. They can provide you a complete sets of training handouts on starting and operating a small business.

This information includes:

- Understanding the Nature of Small Business
- Determining your Potential as an Entrepreneur
- Technical Assistance
- Types Or Ownership
- Marketing Strategy
- Location
- Financing
- Legal Issues
- Government Regulations
- Business Planning
- Management
- Records
- Other

For more information contact the Small Business Administration in your area, or write, U. S. Department of Small Business Administration Washington, DC: U. S. Printing Office. Have them send you a list of their publications. You may also contact The National Center For Research In Vocational Education— The Ohio State University, Columbus, Ohio.

Know what problems you will face before you start out, and get the information and training first.

Good Luck!

MARKETING STUDY PACKAGE

CLIENT:_____

DATE:_____

_____

238

PERSONAL GUIDELINES

TIMING: AN IMPORTANT KEY

* P.O. BOX (only open for 3 weeks)
* Ads (Sunday - Tuesday or Wednesday)
* Note: after you see the "ad," wait 7-10 days before mailing
* Follow up cover letters, i.e. "I will call you next week."
* Best time to mail is Thursday or Friday (based on distance)
* Use the weekend to your advantage
* After mailing cover letter, i.e. "I have been in contact with Mr. X. He is   expecting my call."

FOLLLOW-UP SYSTEM:

* NON-COMPUTERIZED:

* a full-size calendar (be able to see one or two months at a time).
* two (2) file boxes marked A - Z and 1 - 31.

*COMPUTERIZED:

* calendar
* set up cross reference system so that you can track your   activity...companies, referrals, meetings, references, follow-up to letters,   meetings, etc.

KNOWING YOUR SCHEDULE:

* SETTING THE MEETING TIME - Tuesday, Wednesday or Thursday

9 - 11 a.m. or 2 - 4 p.m.

* PHONE CONTACT (they are calling and want to see you)

* Set meeting by your schedule (request a good time).

        *   Get good directions - meeting address, cross
streets, color of building,   phone and extension of
meeting place

* Ask who will you be meeting with - name, title, correct spelling, pronunciation, etc. and if there will be anyone else (if yes, get same information).
* Ascertain how long the meeting is scheduled for.
* Ask if there are any meetings scheduled after yours.

ASK QUESTIONS - PROBE FOR INFORMATION

* Who am I speaking with (name, position, how long with the company)?
* Please forward a copy of your financial report to...
* Is the position open due to promotion, expansion, etc.
* Is someone leaving the company?
* What can you tell me about the position?
* Were you promoted to this position?
* Will I be meeting you?
* Does the company promote from within?
* I appreciate all of your help. (If appropriate) I look forward to working with you.

APPLICATIONS:

* May make you late or delay your meeting.
* Tend to highlight liabilities.
* Force you to sit.

If asked, stall (the company is not going to hire your application), i.e.:

* not enough time to complete
* don't have all the information with me that they require
* would be happy to - do you have an envelope so I may return it?
* If pushed:
  - write slow and big
  - leave out $ sign and references (they'll be furnished with mutual interest)
  - highlight skills - use bare information (i.e. please refer to resume OR full/complete information will be provided during the scheduled business meeting)
* In the box asking for salary earnings:

- not relevant
- not applicable
- based on performance
- based on the position's responsibilities
- open OR flexible
- to be discussed

PROBING/OFFENSIVE QUESTIONS

Until we have identified what the interviewer wants, we don't have anything meaningful to offer.

* PROBING...information-gathering questions that are designed to:

        * demonstrate our interest in the company
        * stimulate conversation about the company's needs, problems and opportunities
            which the person who gets the job may be expected to address
        * lead into a R.A.C.E.
        * learn the subtle, perhaps unwritten, requirements for the job

* PROCEDURE

        * First part of question is in the form of a declarative statement and should show   you have done some research.
        * Second part is the question itself, which is short, open-ended, not expressing an   opinion.

        * After the question is asked, listen carefully.
        * Comment as positively as is appropriate BEFORE asking any follow-up   questions.
        * Make a mental note for job requirements as they become apparent in the   answers.

* AS NEEDS ARE IDENTIFIED, use a R.A.C.E. to demonstrate your ability to fill the   needs. The following sample questions could be used in almost any interview   situation; you should supplement this list with questions of your own, based on your assessment of the situation within the interview setting.

        * What's your (the interviewer's) mission? What are you trying to accomplish that   is different from what has been done in the past?
        * How does the position we are discussing fit into (contribute/relate to) your   mission?

* How well are you progressing toward your goals (significant
accomplishments/disappointments)?

* What are the organization's principal opportunities?
Challenges?

* What are you looking to this position to accomplish
over the next 12-18 months?   (specifics: what, when,
where, how and why)?

* What principal skills are you looking for regarding
this position? What technical,   educational or
experience background?

These questions are designed to accomplish one or more objectives:

* define hiring criteria (until we know what the prospective employer wants to do or do
  differently, you have nothing to "sell")

* build rapport by affording the interviewer an opportunity to tell you about the company

* help to set up a R.A.C.E.

The following sample questions could be used in almost any interview situation. This list can be supplemented with questions of your own, based on your assessment of the situation within the interview setting.

* What do you expect an individual in this position to accomplish over the next 6-12
  months?

* What specific goals have been established? What general goals?

* What is the biggest challenge that I would face?

* What are you trying to accomplish that's different from what's been done in the past?
    OR What new thrusts are anticipated?

* How will my position fit into the corporate structure? OR Would you describe the
  reporting system (i.e. formal or informal) that I will be involved in?

* How well is the company progressing toward its goals (have there been significant
  accomplishments/unanticipated problems)?

* What are the 3 major responsibilities of the position as
you see them?

* From those 3...in your opinion...what has your top
priority?

* How are new ideas typically received?

PROBING / DEFENSIVE QUESTIONS

*   Questions designed to provide the information we need to decide whether we want   the job.

*   Questions designed to protect us against making a bad employment decision.

*   Defer until late in the interviewing process (often until after receiving a firm offer)   as it may put the interviewer on the defensive.

WHAT COULD GO WRONG?
WHAT COULD PREVENT US FROM BEING SUCCESSFUL OR ENJOYING THE WORK?

*   What happened to the previous incumbent? His predecessor?

*   How many people have held this position in the last three years?

*   Is there any likelihood that relocation might be required in the foreseeable future?

*   What is the typical career progression or opportunities from this position?

*   What is expected from this position over the next 8-12 months?

*   How will performance be measured?

*   What authority and resources (both manpower and financial) come with this   position (commensurate with the responsibilities and performance expectation)?   Does position have hire/fire authority? Over whom?

*   Whose (functional) support is required to achieve the objectives in this position   (undermining threat)?

*   What is the approval procedure for...(whatever you feel
you need to function   effectively)?

Defensive questions are designed to restrain you from pursuing, or accepting, a position with a company where you would not be happy, or successful, owing to factors beyond your control. Defensive questions should be used selectively (after you and the interviewer are convinced you're qualified for the position and you are sincerely interested in it) and toward the end of the interviewing process - perhaps even after an offer has been tendered.

---

1. IF EXISTING POSITION: What happened to the incumbent? Why? (Try to get
his/her name from another source.) How long has this position been open? What
happened to earlier incumbents?

   IF PRESENTLY FILLED: What is the status of the incumbent? (Why being
replaced? Does he/she know?)

2. What resources (budget and/or manpower) and authority go with this position's
responsibilities? Does position have hire/fire authority? Over whom?

3. How will other organizational elements or support structure effect my ability to
achieve this position's goals? How do they regard this position (their expectations,
past support/confrontation history)? Where does this position fit into the overall
organization?

4. To whom does the position report (one individual with sufficient authority to provide
necessary support)?

5. Who (all) must approve my actions before they become official?

6. In the past, what has been the organization's response to economic down trends?

7. How is performance evaluated (degree of subjectivity)?
How frequently? What are
        some of the benchmarks?

8. What positions might I progress to based on successful
performance in this position?

9. Is the company about to go public? Any indication it
will be sold (or be acquired)?

10. What are the company's sales and profit trends?

PHONE SCRIPT
VERBAL RESUME

"THIS IS WHAT I CAN DO FOR YOU"

Contact your target company...

*   Ask receptionist the name and complete position, title
of the head of the   department you are interested
in and his/her secretary's name.

*   What product or service does the company provide?

*   When calling for the above information...ask to be
transferred to...or call back.

*   Ask secretary, "I would like to speak with
_____."

*   "Recently I have been conducting research to identify
industries and the companies within the
_____ area."
        * "I have identified (yours) as one in which I could
make significant contributions."
        * "I offer proven ability and feel confident that a
personal meeting will be of mutual   interest and
benefit. What will fit your schedule best...mornings or
afternoons?"

IF ASKED...WHAT CONTRIBUTION OR BENEFIT CAN YOU PROVIDE?
(this is what I can do for you):

List three or four of your supporting strengths...i.e. sales
representative...maintenance supervision...sales/marketing
research & development...customer and field service...from
your select industries.

If not asked the above...request a meeting.
        "Would (day) (am/pm) be a good time to meet or would
_____ be
        better for you?"

* Based on response...select alternative days and times - OR
- ask what will be best for you
    and would (secretary's name) schedule that for us?

* Alternate - "When would be a good time to call so we can set up this meeting?"

* NOTE: If no meeting is scheduled or phone date established...send follow-up letter   resume. Start first paragraph with:
        "As discussed during our conversation on
_____, <refer to letter   resume>."

*NOTE: Refer to "Phone Script - follow-up to letters" for other ways to reach target.

FACTORS FOR POSSIBLE NEGOTIATION

There are many forms of compensation other than base salary. The popularity of various methods fluctuates within industries, occupational specialities and the economic environment. Listed below are the major subjects which might be brought up in the course of negotiations.

Mark the items that are important to you and that match your personal goal.

BASE SALARY
SALES COMMISSIONS
BONUS
EXPENSE ACCOUNTS
MEDICAL INSURANCE
DISABILITY PAY
AD&D INSURANCE
LIFE INSURANCE
VACATION TIME
DIFFERENTIAL
COMPANY-SPONSORED VAN POOL
PARKING
GROUP AUTO INSURANCE
MATCHING INVESTMENT PROGRAMS
ANNUAL PHYSICAL EXAM
ATHLETIC CLUB MEMBERSHIP
SEVERANCE/OUTPLACEMENT
TERMINATION AGREEMENT
CPA AND TAX ASSISTANCE
1ST CLASS OVERSEAS TRAVEL
SHORT TERM LOANS
CONSUMER PRODUCT DISCOUNTS
COMPANY CAR
GAS ALLOWANCE
USE OF VEHICLES IN OFF HOURS
STOCK OPTIONS
ETC.
COUNTRY CLUB MEMBERSHIP
LUNCHEON CLUB MEMBERSHIP
DEFERRED COMPENSATION
CONTINUING EDUCATION
INSURANCE BENEFITS AFTER

RELOCATION:

MOVING EXPENSE

COMPANY PURCHASE OF YOUR
  HOME

                    MORTGAGE RATE

MORTGAGE PREPAYMENT PENALTY

REAL ESTATE BROKERAGE

CLOSING COSTS, BRIDGE LOAN

TRIPS FOR FAMILY TO LOOK FOR
  HOME

LODGING FEES WHILE BETWEEN
  HOMES

SHIPPING OF BOATS AND PETS

INSTALLATION OF APPLIANCES,

MORTGAGE/BRIDGE LOAN

TERMINATION
FINANCIAL PLANNING/LEGAL
ASSISTANCE

THE MOCK INTERVIEW

Business Meeting

APPLICATION: HOW WELL ARE YOU ABLE TO PRESENT (SELL) THE
                              PRODUCT (YOURSELF)?

ASK THE FOLLOWING BASIC QUESTIONS:

1.   ARE YOU CURRENTLY WORKING?

2.   WHAT ARE OR WHAT HAVE YOUR CURRENT EARNINGS BEEN?

3.   WHAT FINANCIAL OFFER WOULD WE HAVE TO MAKE YOU FOR YOU
     TO JOIN OUR FIRM?

4.   EVERYONE HAS PROFESSIONAL LIABILITIES...DO YOU AGREE?

5.   WHAT MIGHT A FEW OF YOURS BE?

6.   WE ARE VERY IMPRESSED WITH YOU...AND TWO OTHER PEOPLE
WE   HAVE MET. WHY SHOULD WE SELECT YOU OVER THEM?

_____

THE 3 TO 5 & 8 TO 12 STRATEGY

DECISION MAKERS:

ON THE AVERAGE MUST BE CONTACTED 3 TO 5 TIMES BEFORE
MAKING A DECISION.

HOW DO YOU ACCOMPLISH THIS?
_____

1.   BROADCAST LETTER

2.   PHONE FOLLOW-UP, RESULTS IN...

     A)   SEND ME MORE MATERIAL?

     B)   PHONE FOLLOW-UP (TO SEE IF MATERIAL WAS RECEIVED)

     C)   SET UP BUSINESS MEETING

     D)   FOLLOW-UP LETTER TO THE MEETING

     E)   PHONE FOLLOW-UP TO LETTER

     F)   SET ANOTHER MEETING

3.   SET UP BUSINESS MEETING

4.   FOLLOW-UP LETTER TO THE MEETING

5.   PHONE FOLLOW-UP TO LETTER

6.   SET ANOTHER MEETING

DECISION MAKERS:

ON THE AVERAGE MUST SAY "YES" 8 TO 12 TIMES BEFORE THEY
WILL MAKE A MAJOR DECISION (MAKE AN OFFER).

THE MEETING DAY

*   DRESS CODE...blue or gray suit (standard business uniform)...white shirt/blouse,   matching or contrasting tie...Dress for Success.

*   BRING TWO COPIES OF RESUME...a minimum of six personal references (on   a separate sheet).

*   CARRY A THIN PORTFOLIO...with a pad.

*   DON'T BE LATE...FIVE TO TEN MINUTES EARLY.

*   AT RECEPTIONIST/SECRETARY, INTRODUCE YOURSELF:

-    My name is _____.
-    My appointment is with _____at _____a.m./p.m. I am a few minutes early, however, please   announce that I am here. Thank you. DO NOT MOVE UNTIL THE   CALL IS MADE.
-    Remain standing - you look better.
-    Use your time...read financial report, letters/awards, review product or sales   hand-outs.

*   THE TWELVE "DO'S" OF EACH MEETING (IN THIS ORDER)...TO BE   ACCOMPLISHED AT THE BEGINNING OF EACH MEETING:

-    tell them who you are
-    tell them why you are there (the position)
-    pay a "business complement"...only
-    this is what I can do for you...a "brief" summary of your background   directed toward the position
-    start asking "OFFENSIVE...PROBING" questions

-    I like the people
-    I like the company
-    I like the position
-    I would like to work for (this company) you

257

*   TO ESTABLISH THE DAY AND TIME OF THE NEXT MEETING

     -      I would like to meet again..would _____ be
good for you or would
          _____ be better?
     -      When is the best time to call...would you prefer a
follow-up call in the   _____ or
_____...what is best for you?
     -      Send within 24 hours (max. 48 hours) A FOLLOW-UP
LETTER to each   person you met highlighting primary
points of the meeting.

     * NOTE: If their answer to your questions was: "no
meeting"..."don't call" -
               CALL ANYWAY...COMPANIES LIKE POLITE,
               AGGRESSIVE, BUSINESS-MINDED PEOPLE WHO
WANT   TO WORK FOR THEM.

     * NOTE: CALL AFTER EACH FOLLOW-UP LETTER.

PERFORMANCE APPRAISAL
(SEMI-ANNUAL)

SECTION I

NAME _____ DATE

CLASSIFICATION

_____

OVERALL PERFORMANCE RATING

_____

SECTION II   List Major Job Duties

1.

_____

_____

_____

2.

_____

_____

_____

3.

_____

_____

SECTION III

    For each factor below, select the definition that best
describes the staff member's performance and   circle the
numerical rating above each.

_____

FACTOR

1.   QUALITY OF WORK - Consider neatness, accuracy, and
general efficiency.

                        (1)   (2)   (3)
                (4)   (5)
        Makes too Accuracy of   Completes   Accuracy is
        Is extremely
        many errors   work is   assignment
        consistently accurate in
        in performing marginal. with a minimum above average.
        tasks. Quality
        tasks. Quality   Usually   follow-up by
            of work is
        of work is   requires   supervisor.
        exceptional.
        unacceptable. additional
                checking.

COMMENTS:

_____

_____

_____

2.   QUANTITY OF WORK - Consider quantity of work turned out
and promptness with which it is
completed.

                (1)   (2)   (3)
    (4)   (5)
        Is too slow. Produces at   Performs Performs tasks
        Exceptionally

260

Productivity   acceptable   assigned tasks with good
high, superior
in tasks is   level in some   promptly. results.
     output in
below   areas. Needs Completes Volume is
performing tasks.
minimum   close super-   expected high and
standards.   vision in order   volume of utilizes
time
                to complete   work.   well.
                assignments.

COMMENTS:
_____

_____

_____

3.   JOB KNOWLEDGE - Consider information and know-how about work duties.

(1)	(2)	(3)	(4)
			(5)
Limited know-	Lacks some	Good know-	Has very
how and	know-how	how; thorough	know-how know-how
knowledge	and know-	knowledge of	and know- and know-
of work duties.	ledge of work	all phases of	ledge
	duties. May	job.	of work ledge of all duties.
	need additional	Comprehends	Extreme work duties.
	Excellent	instructions	difficulty
	training in	and	Comprehends
	some areas.	procedures.	understanding
			ability to
			procedures with
			grasp all ideas
			instructions. explanations.
			and methods.

COMMENTS:

_____

_____

_____

4.   STAFF RELATIONS - Consider the extent to which the staff member cooperates and assists co- workers and superiors.

(1)	(2)	(3)	(4)
			(5)
Unwilling to	Unusually	Works well	Shows
assist others	assists others	with others	Is excellent
and take	and goes out		willingness
directions.	and takes	to provide	of
Uncooperative.	direction. May	directions.	way to
	cooperate and	Always	assistance.
	occasionally		Alert to
	provide		needs

have problems   cooperative   of unit.
Quick.   assistance.
             in this area.   to respond.   Works
well

                                                 with those on
                                                 same level and
                                                 higher levels.

COMMENTS:

_____

_____

_____

SECTION IV

Overall Job Performance Summary. (Include comments that
substantiate the basis for factor ratings. Comment on
performance strengths, weaknesses and suggestions for
improvement and future goals.)

_____

_____

_____

_____

_____

_____

_____

_____

SECTION V

Staff member's comments on Performance Appraisal. You may
also comment, if you wish, on any other job-related matter.

_____

_____

_____

_____

_____

_____

_____

References

How To Sell Yourself, Joe Girard
Simon & Schuster, Inc., A Warner Book

What Color is Your Parachute?, Richard Nelson Bolles
Ten Speed Press

Rites Of Passage, John Lucht
The Viceroy Press

Who's Hiring Who, Richard Latrop
Ten Speed Press

Finding Your Ideal Job, Richard N. Diggs
Progresssive Publications

Jobs '95, Kthryn and Ross Petras
Simon & Schuster, A Fireside Book

RESUMES that KNOCK 'EM DEAD, Martin John Yate
Bob Adams, Inc.

BUSINESS TODAY Fifth Edition, Rachman Mescon
Random House

The Management Of HUMAN RESOURCES. David J. Cheeinton
Allyn & Bacon, A Division of Simon & Schuster, Inc.

Sales Management, Dan H. Robertson & Danny N. Bellenger
Macmillan Publishing Co., Inc.

Glossary Of Term

A

Absenteeism: Not show continuously for you work This negative practice is detrimental in acquiring a job as well as keeping it. .

Agency: In this case an agency is a typically a non-profit organization such as a school district, police department, and county office.

Age Discrimination in Employment Act 1967: Federal legislation requiring employer to treat applicants and employees equally, regardless of age.

Application: Application (Job) this is a document supplied by the employer in which you will supply your employment history and vital personal data as described by law.

Articles of partnership: a document that states explicitly the rights and duties of partners.

Assets: Intangible skills that have economic value in help achieve your new employment.

B

Black List: A list developed by management of undesirable worker or employee to thaw employee in there organization. This information or list may be pass on to other employers. A prepared and rehearsed presentation.

Body (of a letter): The main part of the letter.

Business Plan: A structural plan that is designed to help the businessman or employer consider alternatives that best meet the needs of the company or organization.

Bonus: Cash payment in addition to the regular wage or salary, hence serves as a reward for achievement.

Business cycle: Fluctuations in the rate of growth that an economy experiences over a period of several years.

Budget: A definite plan for saving and spending income.

266

C

Canned: A prepared and/or rehearse presentation. Normally associated with telephone sales. You may want to develop his kind of job search technique if you are doing job search cold calls.

Champion: An individual that will that you can enlist how would be willing to help you get a job by enhancing your image and promoting your cause.

Combination Resume: Has elements from other forms of resumes. General it does not have an occupational goal state.

COBRA: This is a federal legislated Health Benefit that you can subscribe to while you are un-employed. Asked your employer to provide you will information on this benefit. You will have to your share of the fees for your benefit. In some cases you may have to pay both the fee you pay plus the payment that your ex-employer was paying since you are no longer an em-ployee.

Commodity: A valuable product. You must recognize that you have something to offer. But realize you will also be in competition with others. You want to sell yourself to the highest bid-der, but the employer is looking for the people with the best overall skills and can best fit there organizational needs.

Competition: People you will be going up against during your job search.

Compensation: Payment of employees for their work.

Contract: Exchange of promises enforceable by law.

Creativity: You have to be able to see problems as opportunities.

Cross-training: Expanding your knowledge or experience that would make you more valuable to a company or organization. As an example, being able to do more than one job or have the skills to work in another department.

Corporation: Legally chartered enterprise with most of the legal rights of a person, including the right to conduct a business, to own and sell property, to borrow money, and to sue or be sued.

D

Downsized: Being laid off from work do to no fault of your own. Usually association to companies trying to reduce employees to become more efficient. However this may not necessarily be true. The company may have other agendas.

Direct mail: Advertising (resume & employment packet) sent directly to employment prospect through the U.S.Postal Service or by private carriers.

Division of labor: Specialization by workers in performing certain portions of a total job.

E

Effectiveness: Doing the right things in your job search campaign.

Efficiency: Exceeding the minimum about of work for the least amount of pay.

Expense item: All cost associated with job search may be deducted from your income tax responsibility. Remember to keep documentation in case it is required the IRS.

Entrepreneurs: People who organize and develop a business to produce or sell goods and services and are willing to risk failure.

Electronic Mail (E-Mail): text messages transmitted from one computer to another.

F

Family business: Ownership or involvement of two or more family members in the life and functioning of a business.

Feedback: Getting information back with regard to how effective your resume, cover letter are. It is also beneficial to get feedback from how you interview performance is.

Franchisee: Person or group to who a corporation grants an exclusive right to the use of its name in a certain territory, usually in exchange for a initial fee plus monthly royalty payments.

Fringe benefits: Compensation other than wages, salaries, and incentive programs.

Functional Resume: Concentrates on your job skills, abilities, qualificants an what you have done under individual headings.
Fraud: The act of deceiving or misrepresenting yourself. As you fill out your resume or job application remember you can be dismissed from employment for misrepresenting information.

G

Gatekeeper: The gatekeeper is a person such as a secretary or receptionist who is place between the general public as a buffer to control who is allow to see busy executives.

General expenses: Operation expenses, such as office and administrartive expenses. Not directly associated with creating or marketing a good or services

Goals: Targets or your aims.

Goal setting: The successful entrepreneur strives to make things come true.

H

Headhunter: Individual or agent working for a job search company. The company or individual receives fees from the employer or you for placing in a job.

Human Relation Department: Organization within a company involve in screen and hiring of new employees. Also involved in outplacement.

Human skills: Skills required in order to understand other people and to interact effectively with them.

I

Incentives: Cash payments to workers who produce at a desired level or whose unit produces at a desired level.

J

Job analysis: Process by which jobs are studied to determine the task and dynamics involve in performing them.

Job Hopper: One is labeled a job hopper because of short time are on their jobs.

Job Instruction Training: A system designed to make on-the-job training more effective.

K

Key: The most important element in accomplishing an idea or process. In this case most efficient way of finding a job is through "Networking".

L

LIFO: Last in first out. Method of pricing inventory under which the cost of the last goods acquired are the first costs to be charged to cost of goods sold. Sometimes employees will be laid off because the were the last employee to be hired.

Long-range plans: Plans geared to a two-tow five-year span and in some cases longer.

M

Marketing Plan: This is an important document that presents steps in helping the businessman or organization seek the best alternatives to promote the company or firm. On some occasions you may be ask to present a mini-marketing letter to show your planning "savvy".

Management: Process of coordinating resources to meet an objective.

Moonlighting: An employee working more than one job.

N

Networking: Talking to friends, neighbors, business contacts, church members, and club members asking them for help finding someone who might know where there is a position or job. From 64% to over 74% of jobs are gotten through networking. In networking you are looking for referrals from your contacts.

. A pay system that discriminates same skilled employees based
efits for newly hired employees over seasoned and over employee

gnized   to only be able to do one type of skill, industry, or job. Sam
ed".

U

ser extent, those who quit their jobs.

: People believe that they are of less value than they really are.

ment insurance: Government sponsored program for assisting worker who are
d, to a lesser extent, those who quit their jobs.

V

ue: Making yourself more qualified by getting more education, training, or skills.

enture capitalist: Investment specialists who provide money to finance new businesses i
exchange for portion of ownership, with the objective of making a profit.

Voice mail: a computerized system for storing telephone messages.

W

Wages: Cash payment based on a calculation of the number of hours the employee has
worked or the number of units he or she has produced.

Wants: Those things that are not necessary to survival but that make life much more enjoy-
able.

Web page: A location on the Internet placed there by a company, organization, or individual to promote companies, jobs, products, and services.

Work rules: Policies during collective bargaining that govern what type of work union
members will do and the conditions under which they will work.

N

Newsletter: A job search tool used to present some of your special interest, successes, and
achievements that don't show up on your resumes or cover letter.

Needs: Things that humans must have to survive.

Networking: Talking to friends, neighbors, business contacts, church members, and club members asking them for help finding someone who might know where there is a position or job.
From 64% to over 74% of jobs are gotten through networking. In networking you are looking
for referrals from your contacts.

Newsletter: A job search tool used to present some of your special inteerest, successes, and
achievements that don't show up on your resumes or cover letter.

O

Outplacement: A service offered by some employers to transition from their laid off position
to job search or to a new job. Outplacement assists with resumes, phone, job search training
and supplies. Outplacement may be internal or contracted.

Oxymoron: A figure of speech in which opposite or contradictory ideas or terms are combined.

Output per man-hour: The amount of goods that one worker, on the average, can produce in
one hour.

P

Payoff: Payoff here is having that potential employer will you for the interview after you have
consistent in your promoting yourself through self-advertising.

Perks: Special class of fringe benefits made available to an employee by a company for being
valuable.

Pigeon-holed: Being recognized as only being able to working in one industry, field, or job
skill.

Pruning: Pruning a new "buzz" word for being laid off, or "downsize". In theory Pruning like

Partnership: An association of two or more persons operating business as co-owners and sharing profits or losses.

Pigeon-holed: Being recognized as only being able to working in one industry, field, or job skill.

Personality: The qualities of a person that make an impression upon other people.

Pruning: Pruning a new "buzz" word for being laid off, or "downsize". In theory Pruning like downsizing, or "rightsizing" is designed to help a firm or organization to become more efficiency and perhaps profitable.

Punctuality: Being always on time. This is a very good trait you will want to maintain and continue.

Q

Qualified: Verified as having the need, the means, and the authority to make a purchase.

Quotas: Fixed limits on the quantity of as to who is going to be hired.

R

Relocation: Being willing to move to a new area, city, state, or country as part of an employment offer or package.

Resume: Summary of education, working experience, interest, and other personal information.

Risk: The chance that a situation may end with loss or misfortune.

S

Savvy: Having knowledge about an operation or skill. As an example, being computer savvy. Your understand of the subject.

Salaried worker: An employee who earns a stated amount for a given period of tem regardless of the number hours worked.

Severance packages: A compensation package or arrangement given to employees being downsized or laid-off. May be given to an employee to avoid bitterness or a lawsuits. Not all

companies will offer this terminat

Self-confidence: You must feel no t

Short range plans: All individuals should specific period of time.

Script: This is planned presentation that you deve when calling an executive of a potential employer.

SIC: SIC is a code that manufactures, marketing companie uses to identify products and materials being sold or made. into groups by the product they make or market.

Stopgap: Referring to a job or business opportunity which can provic that career position

S corporation: Corporation with no more than 35 shareholders that may be t ship.

Sole proprietorship: A business owned by one person.

T

Tabloid: A newspaper normal published by various industries which has information about new products, organization, as well as sometime jobs within its industry.

Target Market: A target market is the employers, industries, companies that you are planning or will be planning to go after for employment.

Technical skills: Ability to perform the mechanics of particular job.

Tough-mindedness: The entrepreneur must be able to make and stick to decisions.

Willing to take risks: You must be able to take chances based upon intelligent limits.

Window of Opportunity: A job opportunity or business opportunity that suddenly develops all most overnight that you must decided to take action on quickly.

Y

Yellow-dog contract: Agreement forcing workers to promise, as a condition of employment, not to join or remain in a union.